S0-BKT-982

VICTORIAN POTTERY

THE VICTORIAN COLLECTOR SERIES

General Editor: HUGH WAKEFIELD

Keeper of the Department of Circulation, Victoria and Albert Museum

To be published in this Series

VICTORIAN PORCELAIN by Geoffrey A. Godden

VICTORIAN COSTUME by Anne Buck

VICTORIAN EMBROIDERY by Barbara Morris

VICTORIAN POTTERY by Hugh Wakefield

VICTORIAN SILVER AND SILVER PLATE by Patricia Wardle

VICTORIAN GLASSWARE by Betty Bradford

VICTORIAN JEWELLERY by Shirley Bury

ETC.

VICTORIAN POTTERY

By

HUGH WAKEFIELD

Keeper of the Department of Circulation, Victoria and Albert Museum

THOMAS NELSON & SONS
NEW YORK

Published in the United States by
Thomas Nelson & Sons
Library of Congress Catalog Card Number 62-17803
1962

Printed in Great Britain

ACKNOWLEDGEMENTS

MOST of the illustrations for this book I have obtained, gratefully, from the Victoria and Albert Museum. My thanks are, however, also due to the administrators of ten other museums and institutions and to nine private individuals and firms, who have very kindly allowed me to illustrate pottery in their possession or to use their photographs. The name of the owner appears on each caption and, unless otherwise stated, the photographs belong to the owners of the pottery.

Two of those contributing photographic illustrations have also given valuable help in other ways: Mrs. Betty Bradford has drawn two of the line illustrations and the marks in Appendix VIII, and Mr. Geoffrey Godden has read my manuscript and has contributed largely to the information in Appendix II.

I would like to use this opportunity to record my gratitude to the late Peter Floud, my predecessor as Keeper of Circulation in the Victoria and Albert Museum, who conceived the idea of the Museum's centenary exhibition of 1952 on the 'Victorian and Edwardian Decorative Arts', and who thereby set me and several others to work systematically on the problems of the period.

CONTENTS

LIST OF PLATES

LIST OF LINE ILLUSTRATIONS

VICTORIAN POTTERY

INTRODUCTION

IT IS perhaps self-evident that in a volume of this size one could scarcely attempt to review all the multifarious pottery wares of Queen Victoria's reign. This was an age which loved novelty for its own sake and which regarded variety as a virtue. The industrial revolution was ensuring that even the humblest families were able to use modestly decorated pottery for domestic purposes and, in consequence, the number of potteries and the number of their wares were increasing rapidly. Factual details about them can be found in embarrassing quantity in specialist journals, in factory records and in contemporary books such as Llewellynn Jewitt's *Ceramic Art of Great Britain*; but as yet we are scarcely far enough removed from the period to assess the mass of details from a strictly historical viewpoint.

In this volume the author discusses eleven different topics under chapter headings. The topics chosen are naturally ones which are of interest to collectors, or which the author wishes to recommend to collectors. In their choice and arrangement they represent also the main trends in British ceramics during the period, but it will be realised that this method does imply that some wares may be discussed in some detail while others of a broadly similar style may scarcely achieve a mention. So far as possible, the author has avoided any attempt to group wares according to their aesthetic qualities. We are still uncertain of wares which we find ugly, although the point has been reached at which we can with some confidence record our discovery of beauty.

From the collecting point of view the nineteenth-century wares are particularly attractive because they can be collected easily. They have survived in great quantities, even unsuspected, in our own homes; and collections of great potential value for the history of the decorative arts can be formed, often at a negligible cost. It is hoped that collectors will find in this book sufficient suggestions as to subject-matter, together with some basis for distinguishing between the significant and the insignificant. Further information has been given in the appendices which may help to indicate the scope of a subject or will enable the collector to identify individual pieces. Pottery marks, however, are given only when they seem particularly relevant or when they include new information. Nineteenth-century marks on pottery are both more numerous and more self-explanatory than those of the eighteenth century; for this reason no attempt has been made to include an exhaustive list such as is to be found in J. P. Cushion's and W. B. Honey's *Handbook of Pottery and Porcelain Marks*. In this respect the pottery collector is in a different position from that of the porcelain collector, to whom factory marks are far more often a means to an exact knowledge of the decoration and date.

In this series of books porcelain and pottery have been treated as separate subjects. The appeal of porcelain, or china, with its fine translucent body, is clearly distinct from the appeal of all the other ceramic bodies of earthenware and stoneware. Porcelain and pottery are, in fact, only in danger of being confused where the latter seeks to imitate the former; it is perhaps a measure of the nineteenth-century distinction between the two that in this book it is only the chapter on painted pottery which meets at all closely with the contents of Mr. Geoffrey Godden's parallel work on *Victorian Porcelain*.

In compiling the first two chapters extensive use has been made, for the first time, of the records of the Patent Office Design Registry. This source of information has some limitations: one cannot be quite sure that a registered pattern was produced in quantity; and the illustration of a three-dimensional object in the records may be misleading to the extent that it shows only one side of the object registered. The records provide a much larger corpus of documented information about printed and relief patterns than could be available from the study of existing collections, but it should be borne in mind that in this context the author has not necessarily sighted manufactured examples of the patterns to which he refers.

The illustrations naturally follow the subjects of the chapters and have the same effect of concentrating attention upon chosen topics. The objects illustrated are mostly in public museums, but with a few exceptions they have been chosen as normal examples such as the collector may expect most easily to find.

CHAPTER 1

PRINTED POTTERY

THE pre-Victorian part of the nineteenth century saw the development in England and Scotland of many popular styles of decorated pottery. Lustre-decorated pottery had a great vogue in the first four decades of the century; to the same period belongs the brown saltglazed jugs and fancy flasks, and the 'mocha' ware with its creeping liquid decoration on a thin slip. Inevitably such wares continued into Victoria's reign, but, for the most part, they continued with little originality in the styles which had already been set in an earlier period. To the collector lustre ware and mocha ware are essentially pre-Victorian subjects, even though many of the pieces he acquires may have been made considerably later than 1837.

Transfer-printed pottery, however—the sort which is familiarly known as "blue and white"—was one early nineteenth-century ware which not only survived into Victorian times but was being actively developed until at least the middle of the century. Hitherto the interest of collectors has been concentrated upon the styles of transfer-printed pottery which were characteristic of the eighteen-twenties, but it will be found that the new designs of the 'thirties and 'forties reflected the changing sensibilities of the time, and are for that reason a worthy subject for study and for collecting.

Transfer-printed pottery is pottery which has been decorated by the transfer of a pattern from an engraved metal block. The pattern was engraved on the block as a series of lines or dots cut into the metal surface. It was covered with the colouring matter, and wiped to leave the colour only in the engraving. The pattern was then transferred by means of a piece of paper which was pressed on the engraved block and then applied to the surface of the vessel to be decorated. The process could be used on either a pottery or porcelain vessel, and it could be used either before or after the vessel was glazed. Underglaze printing was preferred to overglaze, because the glaze would preserve the decoration from wear; on the other hand, it was difficult to avoid some slight blurring of the lines in a pattern when the glaze was fused over it. A slight blurring of line is, however, a technical limitation which seems to add attraction and character to the traditional "blue and white". Blue was the colour originally associated with the ware, because in the early stages blue derived from cobalt was the only colour which would with certainty survive the temperature needed to fuse the overlying glaze.

The process of transfer printing had been known since the middle of the eighteenth century, when it seems to have been first used in Liverpool; it was much used in the later eighteenth century on porcelain, and for the overglaze decoration of the new cream-coloured wares. The development of underglaze printing on pottery, however, belongs mostly to the nineteenth century. The international fame and prosperity of the English pottery industry was based on the eighteenth-century cream-coloured wares, but this was greatly reinforced by the remarkable success of transfer-printed pottery in the early nineteenth century. In the second and third decades especially, a considerable international trade was established in this cheaply produced and attractive ware. It was made in Staffordshire by almost every pottery firm and by a number of firms elsewhere.

One use of the technique of underglaze printing was for making outline patterns which were subsequently filled with overglaze enamel colours. A mid-Victorian example of the use of this convenient method of decoration is the Brownfield service illustrated in Plate 10. It may be noticed, too, that the underglaze-printing technique was used for producing the celebrated "Willow pattern" of Chinese inspiration, which was originally used at Caughley on porcelain about 1793 and became the most long-lasting and widely known of all patterns on transfer-printed pottery.

The main interest, however, in transfer-printed pottery was its use for purely pictorial patterns. The popular interest of pictures on pottery was bound to be exploited as soon as printing methods could be used on a popular scale. The result was a style of pottery in which considerations of usefulness or attractiveness tended to be outweighed by the pictorial interest of the printing; this is perhaps borne out by the great preponderance of plates and dishes among the surviving transfer-printed wares rather than cups and saucers, teapots and tureens. A huge popular market at home and abroad was ready to enjoy at a slight extra cost the printed illustrations on flat ware, whether they be scenes of local interest or of exotic appeal.

One feature of transfer-printed pottery of particular interest to collectors is the use of backstamps. These are small printed devices on the underside of pieces of pottery which announce the name of the main decoration or of the series to which it belongs. The device is always a decorative one and the name might, for instance, appear on a ribbon spanning a bouquet of flowers. Normally the initials of the maker will also appear on the backstamp and can be identified from the list given in Appendix II. Often, too, the backstamp will state the maker's trade name for the ware he is producing. This might be "Stone China", "Ironstone China", "New Stone", "Semi-porcelain", "Opaque Porcelain", "Granite ware" or "Kaolin ware". Between such names there is often very little technical distinction, and for the most part they are merely individual names for the hard earthenware body which had appeared in Staffordshire in the early part of the nineteenth century and was generally used thereafter for transfer printing.

In the second and third decades of the century, when the market for transfer-printed wares was being developed, most of the printing was carried out heavily in a deep blue colour. The stippled or closely lined dark areas of a print appeared usually as areas of mottled colouring. Most of the subjects were topographical; but it is interesting to notice that the greatest number of these were American scenes catering for an important market which the English potters had found in the United States. Potters such as Enoch Wood & Sons, James & Ralph Clews, and John & William Ridgway produced some hundreds of American views taken from contemporary topographical prints. Often the prints were chosen for their exotic appeal, as in the case of the Indian sporting scenes which were used by both Josiah Spode and J. & R. Clews; sometimes the appeal was both topographical and exotic, as in Spode's "Caramanian" series; sometimes the prints were taken from paintings with a story interest, as in J. & R. Clews's "Dr. Syntax", "Don Quixote", and "Wilkie" series. The borders around the pictorial scenes were mostly made up of large-scale units; these usually included groupings of large flowers, but in the well-known instance of Enoch Wood & Sons' American scenes the border normally used was one based on an arrangement of sea shells.

Against this background the printed pottery of the 'thirties and 'forties can be distinguished by the cumulative effect of a number of changes in style and in technique. The increased use of colours other than blue will be discussed later, although it should be noticed here that blue continued to be by far the most popular colour. The printing now tended to be lighter and therefore to show more detail than the earlier prints, although this cannot be stated as more than a general tendency. Changes in technique and also in style can perhaps be checked most clearly in the work of the Spode factory, which had been associated more than any other with the production of "blue and white". In 1833 the firm's title was changed to Copeland & Garrett, and in 1847 it was again changed when the name Garrett was removed from the title; so far as marked pieces are concerned there is therefore an automatic distinction between those made before and after each of these dates.

Naturally the more popular of the old designs continued in use for many years and, in particular, one often finds the well-known Spode designs with the mark of "Copeland & Garrett"; but in the new designs of the time the subject-matter seems to take on a new significance. The old designs had nearly always been taken from other sources, sometimes copied directly and sometimes adapted to suit the purpose of pottery decoration. It was difficult for manufacturers to avoid basing the representation of topographical subjects on existing prints, especially when the subjects were on the other side of the Atlantic; but by the middle 'thirties topographical subjects were losing popularity, and many motifs were being designed especially for the purpose of printing on pottery. Clearly the extent of the trade had brought into existence a new breed of artist-craftsmen who could do much more than copy and adapt existing prints, and the upshot was that the design of printed pottery became for the first time an art in its own right, independent both of textile printing and of book illustration. For the collector this means that the early Victorian printed designs are more likely to be satisfactory in a ceramic sense, and that they are more likely to preserve the flavour of their period than the earlier ones which originated in prints intended for a less decorative purpose.

Many of the designs ascribed to the 'thirties are fanciful scenes, which may include copied elements but are only slightly connected with topographical reality. Plate 1 shows a dish with a "Venetian" subject which is fictional in every sense except that it evokes an idealised concept of the Venetian scene; its appeal is entirely that of a decorative drawing with sentimental or romantic overtones. This was the period of popular romanticism, and on printed pottery this nearly always took the form of idealised landscapes built up of consciously picturesque elements.

The borders used for the new designs of the 'thirties, and to some extent those of the later 'twenties, show a remarkable increase in the use of rococo motifs. These consist mostly of asymmetrical arrangements of leafage scrolls, such as can be seen accompanying the fanciful Venetian scene on Plate 1. The historical rococo style belonged to the middle of the eighteenth century; its revival in the nineteenth century was mainly expressed in the exaggeration of certain rococo clichés. The revival seems to have begun in some of the silverwork made for the Prince Regent in the second decade of the century; in porcelain it was expressed a little later in the encrusted flower-work of Coalport and other factories; and during the 'thirties the revived rococo can be considered the dominant and most typical style in almost all of the decorative arts excepting glassware.

From 1839 it was possible for manufacturers to register new designs with the Patent Office and thereby obtain for a time the exclusive right to use them. The records associated with these registrations provide useful information on the subsequent history of printed pottery, with regard both to the history of the firms who were concerned in the trade and to the stylistic developments which are expressed in the new designs. It should be remembered, however, that firms would only be inclined to register designs which they thought might be pirated, and it is clear that some firms were much more sensitive to this possibility than others. At Appendix III is a list of firms which registered scenic printed designs up to 1870. Extensive use was being made of printing for many different ceramic purposes and therefore, in order to define this list as exactly as possible, account has only been taken of those registrations which were made in the form of a print for a plate or dish and which show in the centre a scenic design; wholly floral or foliage designs have been excluded, but a central design depicting a group of pottery has been allowed. Pieces bearing a registered design were most often marked to that effect; from 1842 to 1883 a lozenge-shaped registry mark was used and the code for interpreting this is explained in Appendix I.

Of the designs registered in the 'forties and 'fifties surprisingly few are recognisably topographical. J. K. Knight & G. Elkin of the Foley Potteries seem to have issued a series called "Baronial Halls"; one of these was registered in 1844 and depicts Cobham Hall, complete with figures in costume and a strapwork border. Also in 1844 William Ridgway & Son of Hanley issued an ambitious Alpine lake scene which is presumably derived from an already existing drawing or print. But by far the greater part of the pictorial prints of this period were scenes of the purest fantasy, which taken as a group provide an intimate image of early Victorian ideals. Superficially the range of title and subject-matter is wide, but the common denominator of these fanciful scenes is firm enough to constitute a clearly defined style. Most of them show water overhung by trees with distant buildings, neo-gothic châlets or ruins; often there is a bridge in the middle distance, a boat or two with figures and a stairway leading down to the water (Plates 3, 4). Most of these designs were given names which appear on the backstamps. Many of the names are geographical ones, such as "Aleppo" (by Clementson, Young & Jameson, 1844), "Friburg" (by G. Phillips, 1846), "California" (by Josiah Wedgwood & Sons, 1849), "Siam" (by J. Clementson, 1850) and "Byzantium" (by John Ridgway, 1854); but in such instances the name has no connection with the print other than perhaps a slight cast in the architecture of the buildings or the costume of the figures. Reality is only touched when thoroughly familiar buildings form part of the fictional scene, as in the instance of "Windsor" registered by Mellor, Venables & Co. in 1849.

An often repeated motif among these fictitious scenes was a classical vase, or vases, prominently placed in the foreground. An example was the "Medici" pattern of Mellor, Venables & Co., registered in 1847. A print in a similar style, with the title "Warwick Vase", was registered in 1850 by J. & M. P. Bell of Glasgow and was mentioned in the official catalogue of the 1851 Exhibition, although it may be noticed that the Warwick vase by itself had formed the centre of an earlier print from the Spode/Copeland factory (S. B. Williams, *Antique Blue and White Spode*). Often the interest of a design was concentrated upon a simple arrangement of pottery, as in the instances of J. Clementson's "Claremont" of 1856 and designs which were registered in 1862–3 by Eardley & Hammersley, Edward Challinor, Jones & Ellis and Bodley & Harrold. A classical vase appears in the foreground of the scene on the J. T. Hudden example illustrated on Plate 6. Entitled "Bosphorus", this design was probably issued in the 'sixties, but it is interesting to notice that the foreground is virtually an exact copy of the foreground in a design registered by Copeland & Garrett in 1845 (Plate 5).

Probably the strongest concept among the whole group of fanciful designs was that of the Alpine lake. The title of "Lucerne" was given to at least two designs—by J. Clementson in 1842 and by Enoch Wood & Sons in 1845. Scenes with Chinese architectural details were fairly common, such as the one issued by John Ridgway in 1846, with the inappropriate title of "Aladdin", and the example illustrated here by John Rogers & Son (Plate 4); but in this period, when the influence of Chinese ceramics was at a low ebb, the Chinese scenes were not expected to have Chinese borders, and examples are found in which, for instance, a Chinese arrangement of flowers and vases is surrounded by a border of Chinese scenes and European scrolls.

A subsidiary theme was that of rural England, with its cottages and halls, cows and rustic figures. Prints with this sort of appeal had been produced since at least the early part of the century. They had never been very common, but they were perhaps becoming more frequent in the 'forties and 'fifties. Some of them may have been copied from, or suggested by, paintings, but most were probably original works by the same artists as were responsible for the fanciful scenes. Their conception was, however, distinct from that of the fanciful scenes, and they implied more realistic and less water-bound conventions. The rustic scenes might almost be real scenes; the fanciful scenes could never be. A fine Copeland print registered in 1850 showed cows before a half-timbered farm, and another of 1857 showed cows beside a stream. Other examples, which have perhaps more obvious connections with the fanciful scenes, were registered by John Ridgway (1848), by Venables & Baines (1852) and by George Wooliscroft (1853).

The borders of the 'forties and 'fifties were a great deal more diverse than they had been in previous decades. The characteristic decoration of the period showed an extreme eclecticism in the use of motifs from many different styles and periods, coupled with a remarkable lack of inhibition in the creation of new motifs. The combination of new and old, of original and derived, produced a style of popular art which defies definition but is yet highly characteristic. The revived rococo patterns naturally continued, at least into the 'forties, and reached their most elaborate culmination in the Copeland & Garrett "Louis Quatorze" border which was originally registered in 1844 (Plate 5). One group of patterns appearing in the mid-'forties are remarkably subdued, consisting, for instance, merely of a ground of spaced zig-zag lines. Patterns of this sort were issued mostly in conjunction with the more finely engraved of fanciful scenes, and were registered by firms such as John Ridgway and John Meir & Son. A similarly restrained, but distinctive, border pattern consisting of seaweed-like motifs on a reticulated ground was used by William Ridgway & Son (a separate firm from that of John Ridgway). A tendency to divide the border area into strongly marked panels is more characteristic of the later part of the period, especially of the middle and later 'sixties, when an earlier fashion was revived for placing subsidiary scenes within the border panels (Plate 6).

Little is known, or has as yet been rediscovered, about the artists who were responsible for creating the early Victorian scenic designs. A great number of the original drawings for the engravings have been preserved in the Victoria and Albert Museum, but tantalisingly few of them are signed or bear any exact information as to their origin. The production of engravings for transfer printing was specialised work, and very few of the pottery firms are likely to have had their own engraving shops. Normally the making of suitable drawings would go with the work of translating them into engravings, and the specialist firms carrying out this work would sell the finished product to the pottery manufacturers. This is made very clear in the Design Registry books, where two designs which are closely similar in their style, in their technique and even in their border patterns, are registered by different pottery firms, as in the instance of John Meir & Son's "Mazara" and G. Phillips's "Corinth", registered within a few days of the end of 1844 and the beginning of 1845, and in the instance of two scenes with foreground sculpture both registered in 1852 by Marple, Turner & Co. and by John Holland.

The detail of drawing in the fanciful scenes varies between two widely separate extremes. There seems, however, to be some reason for supposing that the variations arose from demands for different qualities of work, rather than from the styles of different groups of artists. On the one hand there are the finely drawn designs in which

1

Blue-printed dish; on reverse are the marks COPELAND & GARRETT LATE SPODE impressed and printed, the latter with the title VENICE; 1833-47. Length $18\frac{7}{8}$ in. *Victoria & Albert Museum.*

2

Minton blue-printed plate. On the reverse is a backstamp PASSION FLOWER and M & CO., the impressed mark 'new stone' and factory date-mark for 1850. Diam. $10\frac{1}{4}$ in. *Victoria & Albert Museum.*

3. Blue-printed plate, with backstamp 'Versailles' and initials (?) B W & B (Batkin, Walker & Broadhurst); 1840-45. Diam. 10½ in. *Victoria & Albert Museum.*

4. Blue-printed soup plate, with backstamp 'Chinese Porcelain' and 'ROGERS' impressed (John Rogers & Son); about 1840. Diam. $9\frac{7}{8}$ in.
Victoria & Albert Museum.

5. Design for a printed plate registered by Copeland & Garrett in 1845. The border, known as 'Louis Quatorze', had been registered alone in 1844.
Patent Office Design Registry.

6.
Black-printed plate, with backstamp 'BOSPHORUS' and initials J T H (John Thomas Hudden); about 1860-65. Diam. $9\frac{1}{4}$ in.
Mrs. Betty Bradford.

7. Blue-printed dish, with backstamp 'Triumphal Car' and J & M P B & Co. (J. & M. P. Bell, Glasgow); about 1850. Length $7\frac{5}{8}$ in. *Mrs. Betty Bradford.*

8
'I see you, my Boy'. Pot lid made by F. & R. Pratt with a colour print by Jesse Austin (signed); about 1850–60. Diam. 4⅛ in. *City Museum, Sheffield.*

9
Pot lid with colour print illustrating the 1851 Exhibitio[n]. Its manufactu[re] is ascribed to T. J. & J. Mayer (H. G. Clarke, *Centenary Pot-li[d] Book*). The design was registered by the food manufacturers Cross[e] & Blackwell in October 1850. Diam. 5¼ in. *City Museum, Sheffield.*

10. Plate with printed and hand-tinted decoration, made by W. Brownfield. The reverse bears an 1862 registry mark, and an inscription stating that the drawings for the service were made by 'Phiz', H. K. Browne. Diam. $9\frac{1}{4}$ in.
Victoria & Albert Museum.

11

Cup and saucer by Mintons; date mark 1856. The blue-printed 'gothic' decoration is by A. W. N. Pugin, and the shapes are those designed by Henry Cole for the service with which he won a silver medal from the Society of Arts in 1846. Ht. of cup 3 in. *Stonyhurst College (Victoria & Albert Museum photograph).*

12. Plate decorated with a photographic print, said to have been made in 1892. The reverse bears the stamp of the London dealers, Mortlocks, and is impressed 'CAULDON' (the pottery of Brown-Westhead, Moore & Co.) Diam. 10 in. *Victoria & Albert Museum.*

the architectural details are well rendered, although the buildings rarely make sense except as follies: in these a group of foreground figures is normal, and staircases leading into the water and ornamental vases are frequent; a good example is the design "Versailles", which is on the plate illustrated here and apparently made by Batkin, Walker & Broadhurst (Plate 3). On the other hand there are the scenes in which the buildings are quite simply drawn, usually with the romantic exaggeration of some dominant feature such as Elizabethan barge-boards or Gothic crockets: examples of this style such as Thomas Dimmock Jnr.'s "Rhine" (1844) or George Phillips's "Friburg" (1846), may consist of little but buildings, trees and water. Some at least of the elaborate fanciful designs, and probably some of the simpler ones, came from the studio of James Cutts of Shelton. This artist, who was the son of John Cutts the ceramic painter, was active from the mid-'thirties to the 'sixties; he is represented in the Victoria and Albert Museum collection by a few fine drawings which are signed by him and are obviously intended for ceramic engraving.

Besides the fanciful scenes and the rustic scenes, occasional use was also made of figure scenes in a pseudo-classical style. The Glasgow firm of J. & M. P. Bell produced prints of this sort on several occasions (Plate 7), and it is interesting to notice that, when the firm of William Brownfield commissioned some designs for printing from the artist H. K. Browne ("Phiz" of *Punch*), the scenes produced, in 1862, were of well-drawn classical figures (Plate 10).

All the styles which have been discussed so far were used for monochrome printing, and mostly for underglaze printing in blue. From the mid-'twenties onwards other colours were being used for underglaze printing, including black and varying shades of green, red, purple, brown and yellow. Blue continued to be by far the most popular colour, but as an alternative any particular design might also be produced in one of the other available colours. A development of the later 'forties was to use a number of colours in succession to produce a colour print. This was the period when George Baxter was developing his method of colour printing on paper, and it was natural that the same idea should be used for pottery. The process as applied to pottery was worked out by Jesse Austin (who had at one time been an independent engraver of pottery designs) and Felix Edwards Pratt at the Fenton firm of F. & R. Pratt (Plate 8).

There was no delay in exploiting the process and, at the 1851 Exhibition, F. &. R. Pratt were able to mount an impressive display of colour-printed pottery which was mainly responsible for earning the firm an "honourable mention" among the jury awards. Other firms had also seized on the possibilities of colour printing and, in the Great Exhibition period, the process was being used by T., J. & J. Mayer of the Dale Hall pottery, and by John Ridgway of the Cauldon pottery. In later years the process continued to be used mainly by Pratts, and to a lesser extent by the successive firms at the Dale Hall and Cauldon potteries. Jesse Austin was an original artist of talent, and of the great number of prints produced by Pratts many are from his own watercolour drawings, besides those which were copied from other sources. The process was used for the decoration of table services and of ornamental pottery such as flower vases; but such wares were mostly made for export to America, and from the beginning the most important use of colour printing in the home market was for the decoration of commercial pot lids (Plates 8 and 9). The pots which were thus embellished were used for toilet preparations and, later, for fish paste and other delicacies. It seems that in its application to this country's needs the process fell between the alternatives of the cheap and expensive markets. The process must have proved too expensive for a popular market such as was being exploited by the monochrome prints; one supposes that by the middle of the century the more sophisticated buyers were less likely to be impressed by the novelty of having reproduced pictures on their pottery. In effect a limited field of compromise was found by using the process to strengthen the attractions of what must have been relatively luxurious potted preparations. The pot lids were however produced in a bewildering variety of designs, especially in the 'fifties and 'sixties, and many of them have been reproduced in later times. For many years they have attracted the keen interest of collectors for their colourful and skilfully rendered designs, and for the insight they give into many aspects of life a hundred years ago. For the would-be collector the fullest information is already available, and more than three hundred different designs have been listed and described in detail.*

By the later 'fifties and 'sixties the popularity of monochrome scenic prints on pottery was clearly declining in this country; the

* H. G. Clarke, *Under-glaze Colour Picture Prints on Staffordshire Pottery*, London, 1949.

same probably applies to the multicoloured prints which, apart from the jar lids, were finding their chief market in America. It is true that there was a sudden increase, about the later 'sixties, in the number of scenic prints registered, but many of these were continental topographical scenes or representations of continental royalty with inscriptions in the languages of the countries concerned. The English potters had apparently found a new market on the Continent and particularly in Eastern Europe. It is curious that some of these designs, presumably for manufacture in this country, were being registered by continental agents from addresses in Birmingham, Liverpool and Cardiff.

With the gradual recession of interest in scenic designs, transfer printing tended more and more to be regarded as merely a cheap means of decorating table wares with floral patterns. A floral design might be used in the centre of a plate in the manner of a scenic design, or, more frequently, the design might consist simply of a floral border pattern. Some of the best of the floral designs are, however, relatively early and are of great beauty. Wedgwood examples are well known in a style of floral pattern which strides boldly over a wide surface. In the mid-'forties a distinctive style of running plant and floral motifs appeared in several different ceramic media; the whole decoration of an object was effected by the representation of one plant, the sprays of which were consciously disposed in relation to the space to be filled (see page 51). On printed wares this style took the form of largely-drawn, semi-naturalistic flower sprays arranged in a deep border. Mintons were perhaps the firm most associated with this style, but similar work was also produced by Copelands, and by such smaller firms as George Phillips of Longport and Thomas Phillips & Son of Burslem, who both registered designs of this sort in 1845. In some of these designs an emphatic outer border was achieved by running the stem of the plant around the outer edge. An attractive example of this arrangement is illustrated here in a plate which bears the Minton date mark for 1850 (Plate 2). Mintons also printed some formal "gothic" patterns designed by the well-known gothic revivalist A. W. N. Pugin about the middle of the century (Plate 11). Such patterns were too austere to be widely popular but, like the running-plant patterns, they are of interest because they belong very precisely to the aesthetic outlook of the mid-century years. In contrast, the most striking patterns of the last quarter of the century, especially of the later 'seventies and 'eighties, were derived from a new enthusiasm for Japanese art; many firms were then producing printed services covered by attractive asymmetrical arrangements of motifs such as bamboo sprays and fans.

One Victorian variety of printed pottery remains to be mentioned. From the early 'sixties onwards, photographs were being used in effect as ceramic decoration by a complicated process which usually involved transferring a film of photographic material on to the ceramic body and firing it under a normal ceramic glaze. Such work has generally the appearance of an experiment, or suggests the personal interests of an individual amateur photographer, who in many cases will have carried out the work. Several firms seem to have experimented with the process, but it seems scarcely to have been developed as a normal mode of decoration for table services. An example from the last decade of the century is shown here, which was made for Mortlocks, the London dealers, and is said to have been photographically processed by a Nottingham chemist before being fired in Staffordshire (Plate 12). It may also be noticed that photographic processes were being used in the last quarter of the century, especially perhaps by Wedgwoods, as a novel means of using drawings as printed decoration.

CHAPTER 2

DECORATIVE JUGS

IT MAY seem strange that for a long period during early and middle Victorian times one particular sort of ceramic vessel, the jug, was considered pre-eminently the subject for relief decoration. It is obvious that jugs were in universal use for table purposes. They were constantly in view and had therefore to be decorated; for this purpose relief decoration was ideal, since it was cheap and the jugs would be given automatically the frequent cleaning that relief decoration needs. For tableware used more intimately, such as cups and plates, this sort of decoration was less suited, since its roughness intruded on the touch; and for more decorative objects, notably flower vases, a relief pattern was regarded as something of a dust-catcher until it was justified by the later vogue for dark-coloured vases of stoneware and terracotta.

The relief-decorated jugs can be regarded as a manifestation of "popular" art, since they were produced in quantity for the widest market. Their decoration was included in the mould from which they were cast, and so scarcely any extra expense was involved beyond that of forming the original model. Relief decoration of this sort is, of course, to be distinguished from that of affixing clay motifs which have already been moulded or modelled elsewhere, as in the case of jasper-ware; it is also to be distinguished from relief decoration which has been carved on the surface, as in the case of the more individual saltglazed stonewares of the latter part of the century.

For the collector the jugs are of peculiar interest since they cover almost every aspect of Victorian design. Many of them are of documentary interest; many are intrinsically beautiful. Nearly all their designs are original and Victorian, if only because the medium was too new to be used for the deliberate imitation of historical styles. Naturally the jugs have survived in great quantities and, for this reason, they provide the collector with the opportunity of making valuable specialist collections. In most cases they are easily identified from a maker's mark on the base, and many of them were registered at the Patent Office Design Registry and bear the appropriate registry mark (see Appendix I). It may be noticed, too, that many of the early jugs and other relief-decorated wares bear the legend "Published by . . ." followed by the maker's name and an exact date, which signifies that a representation of human or animal forms has been entered for protection at Stationers' Hall under legislation dating from the reign of George III.

The jugs were made in many different materials, from brown saltglazed stoneware to parian porcelain, but most typically they were made in the various white and near-white industrial bodies which were elaborated in the early part of the nineteenth century and which approximated to stoneware. Usually the stoneware was fully glazed on the inside, but only lightly glazed on the outer surface; often the body appeared buff-coloured or was coloured blue or bluish green. The ground of the relief pattern was sometimes given a coloured stain in emulation of jasper-ware (Plate 19); and sometimes the relief decoration itself was picked out in colour.

This type of jug first becomes recognisable among the products of the eighteen-thirties. The example by W. Ridgway illustrated in Plate 13 is dated October 1st, 1835, and has nearly all the Early Victorian characteristics of style and technique. Its sharply formed relief decoration cast in the mould, its shaped, upward-flaring lip, its low-weighted body and its well-defined foot, all combine to suggest the basic style of the years between the mid-'thirties and the mid-'forties. It may be noticed, however, that the profile of the period was usually rounded and bulging, except when an angular shape was demanded by the decoration.

In 1847 the Burslem firm of T. & R. Boote registered a "new shape for jugs". This was straight-sided in shape, tapering slightly inwards towards the rim, and was perhaps the starting-point for the "tankard" shape which, over the intervening century or so, has become the commonest utility shape for jugs in both pottery and glass. In the years around the middle of the century a number of the relief-decorated jugs were modelled in this shape or in close variations of it (Fig. 1); subsequently the shape continued to appear at intervals. Sometimes the basic tankard shape was given a foot or a footring; sometimes the rim was flat, although the examples with upward flaring lips were by far the more common.

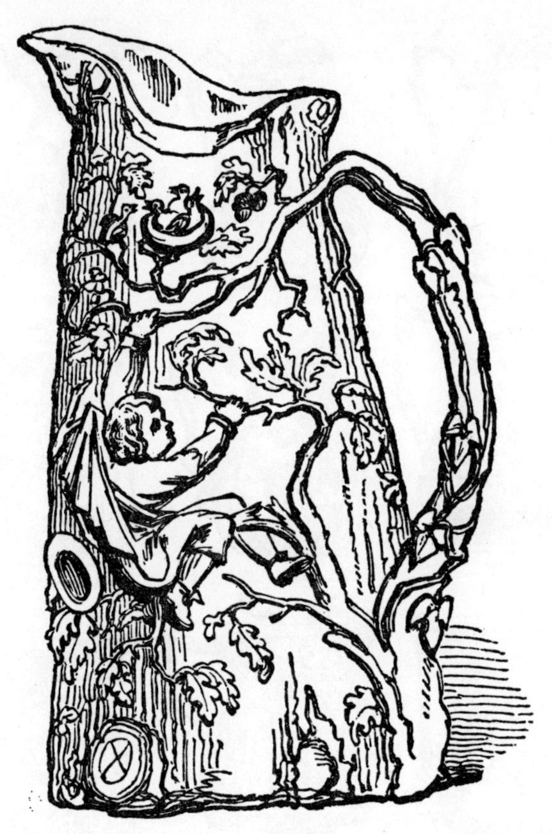

FIG. 1. Jug with decoration of a boy birdsnesting, by T., J. & J. Mayer (*Journal of Design and Manufactures*, 1851).

The rounded, low-bellied jugs continued through the later 'forties, 'fifties, and 'sixties, but in the years about the middle of the century the distinct foot became unusual and a simple footring was normal. Many variations appeared, however, such as the curious cut-away base of the T. &. R. Boote jug illustrated in Plate 14. By the 'seventies and 'eighties the decorative jugs were beginning to lose their identity; but it is worth noticing that by the early 'seventies the bulging belly had in many instances flattened to a slight overhang which approximated almost to a widely based tankard shape on a footring (Fig. 8). and by the later 'seventies and 'eighties a riot of ungainly bizarre shapes had stemmed from the current influence of Japanese pottery.

FIG. 2. Jugs advertised by Cork & Edge in the catalogue of the British Section at the Paris Exhibition of 1855.

13. Jug with scenes from Robert Burns' poem Tam o'Shanter, inscribed on the base *Published by W. RIDGWAY & Co., HANLEY, October 1, 1835.* Ht. $7\frac{7}{8}$ in.
Musées royaux d'Art et d'Histoire, Brussels.

14. White stoneware jug with a scene representing the infant Samuel, made by T. & R. Boote. On the base is a printed registry mark of 1848. Ht. 10 in.
Mrs. Betty Bradford.

15
White stoneware jug with figures in Gothic niches, inscribed on the base *REGISTERED March 17th, 1842, By CHARLES MEIGH, Hanley*. Ht. $6\frac{1}{4}$ in. *Victoria & Albert Museum.*

16
White stoneware jug with jousting figures, inscribed on the base *Published by W. RIDGWAY, SON & Co., HANLEY, September 1, 1840.* Ht. $7\frac{3}{4}$ in. *Mr. Charles Handley-Read.*

17

White stoneware mug with a scene of dancing figures adapted from Nicholas Poussin's painting 'Bacchanalian Dance'. On the base is an inscription recording the presentation of a medal by the Society of Arts to Charles Meigh (in 1847). Ht. $7\frac{1}{4}$ in. *Victoria and Albert Museum.*

18

White stoneware jug w
figures in Gothic niches
registered by T., J. & J
Mayer. 1846. Ht. $8\frac{7}{8}$ i
Mr. Charles Handley-Rea

FIG. 3. Jugs advertised by Cork & Edge in the catalogue of the British Section at the Paris Exhibition of 1855.

Notable among the jugs of the 'forties were those decorated with Gothic detail. A Wedgwood jug of the second decade of the century, with applied figures as well as cast decoration, may perhaps be the precursor of this style (illustrated in Wolf Mankowitz, *Wedgwood*, Fig. 31). In 1840 appeared the well-known jug of W. Ridgway & Son on which jousting knights were depicted under gothic panelling (Plate 16). This jug, like the 1835 one from the same firm illustrated on Plate 13, has its date of publication firmly impressed on the base. The same shape and marginal gothic detail were used on a "stag" jug which appears among the jugs advertised by Cork & Edge in the British Section Catalogue at the Paris Exhibition of 1855 (Fig. 2 and see page 48). But the most famous of the gothic jugs,

FIG. 4. Jug by Charles Meigh & Son (*Art Journal* catalogue of the 1851 Exhibition).

and the one which set the style for most of the others, was registered in 1842 by Charles Meigh. This jug, often known as the "Minister" jug, was vertical-sided and bore a relief figure in each of eight gothic niches (Plate 15). It was obviously a great success and fitted admirably the prevailing sentiments of the 'forties. At the same time Meigh registered an alternative in precisely the same form but without the figures presumably in order to appeal to a different section of religious opinion; four years later a similar version appeared with a representation of the Virgin and Child with St. John the Baptist on each side of the jug (Fig. 4).

Meanwhile other firms were beginning to appreciate the popularity of the gothic motifs. In 1846 T., J. & J. Mayer were registering a pattern of figures in niches which sloped backwards on a tapering jug-shape (Plate 18). In 1848 came T. & R. Boote's curious shape with a biblical scene beneath wide niches (Plate 14). Other variations in the use of gothic niches were the wide-rimmed jug which was registered by Holland & Green in 1854, and another wide-rimmed example, with figures, which was included among those advertised by Cork & Edge in 1855 (Fig. 2); another biblical scene with derived gothic ornament appeared in Samuel Alcock's registration of a "Daniel in the lions' den" motif in 1859.

Inevitably in this age of stylistic eclecticism the gothic jugs were balanced by classical ones; but in this relief-decorated ware classical jugs were no more imitations of classical wares than the gothic jugs were imitations of the truly medieval pottery. Indeed, the classical jugs are only described as such in so far as their decoration includes figures which are classical in origin or in spirit. Usually the figures are combined with loose plant patterns, particularly of vines, and are placed on the typical jug shapes of the mid-century period with their weight well towards the base. In perhaps only one instance, that of a T., J. & J. Mayer jug of 1845 patterned with vines and classical masks, was there any sign of the high-shouldered Greek "oenochoe" jug shape which was being much imitated at the time in other types of pottery. Bacchic scenes were obviously suitable for combining with vine patterns. Charles Meigh introduced a jug in 1844 which was decorated with vines and with a Bacchic scene of dancing figures adapted from Nicholas Poussin's "Bacchanalian Dance" in the National Gallery; and in 1847 he won a medal from the Society of Arts for a mug decorated with the same scene (Plate 17). A similar combination is to be seen in the Silenus jug which was made by Mintons (Plate 19), and which also appeared in brown saltglazed stoneware. Other classical examples included Edward Walley's jug of 1850 with a classical figure group, Thomas Till & Sons' jug of 1854 with a combat scene, and "The Graces" jug which was registered in 1855 by the South Derbyshire firm of Joseph Thompson.

A related group of jugs, vaguely Classical or Renaissance in spirit, made a feature of the naked sexless children which are usually known as *amorini*. Whatever their origin, the children were always represented with a characteristic Victorian playfulness. On a Minton jug of 1845 and on a J. & T. Lockett jug of 1852 they are playing with garlands; on a George Baguley example of 1854 the children are swinging gaily from the pattern on the upper part of the jug. On another Minton example of 1845 they are equipped with wings and are flying spirally up the side of the vessel; and on a jug of 1855 by

F. & R. Pratt they are leaning out of leafage scrolls to shoot at animals with bows and arrows.

All these gothic and classical reminiscences on the cast jugs are charming, but they could not by themselves comprise the whole scope of a truly popular art. Motifs from everyday life—such as may be called genre subjects—had no doubt a stronger appeal to many Victorians, and many of these have the greatest appeal to collectors today, since they carry the flavour of the period in the style of their subjects as well as in their decorative detail.

Sporting scenes and drinking scenes are perhaps the two most frequent genre subjects to be found on the jugs of the 'forties and 'fifties. A jug jointly registered by Edward Walley and by T. & R. Boote in 1845 shows shooting scenes; in 1857 J. & M. P. Bell produced one with stag-hunt scenes, complete with a handle in the form of an antler; and in 1859 a jug by E. & W. Walley was decorated with a representation of hanging game. Another stag-hunt jug appears among the Cork & Edge wares advertised in 1855 (Fig. 2), and this may have originated a decade or so earlier at the pottery of W. Ridgway. Certainly its shape is typical of jugs being designed about 1840, and its incidental detail is virtually identical with that of W. Ridgway's jug depicting jousting knights (Plate 16, and see page 45).

The use of motifs connected with drinking was appropriate since these jugs were no doubt often used, and perhaps mainly used, for serving beer at table. The 1835 example by W. Ridgway, noticed above, included a drinking scene (Plate 13, see page 38), and the same firm registered in 1851 a jug with a similar scene, decorated this time with barley and with a hop vine climbing around the handle. A related theme was used by Henry J. Townsend in his "Hop jug", which was probably the most ambitious of all the mid-Victorian jugs with raised decoration (Plate 20). Henry Townsend was a master at the Government School of Design at Somerset House, and his "Hop jug" is a classic instance of the Victorian conception of suggestive ornament; that is, ornament which by its nature suggests the purpose of the object it adorns. It was made by Mintons, who registered it in 1847; but it was sponsored by Henry Cole, who was later to play an important part in the organisation of the 1851 Exhibition and in the early development of what is now known as the Victoria and Albert Museum. In 1846 Cole had won a silver medal of the Society of Arts for an earthenware tea-service (Plate

11), and in the following year or so he was seeking, under the pseudonymn of Felix Summerly, to improve the standard of the decorative arts by commissioning designs from prominent painters and sculptors for his "Summerly's Art Manufactures". Some attractive pieces were produced under this scheme, but most of them tended perhaps to suggest that good painters and sculptors are not automatically good industrial artists.

Among jugs which carried more general scenes from contemporary life may be mentioned Samuel Alcock's gypsy jug of 1842, also made by one of the Ridgway firms and by Jones & Walley (J. H. Park, *Antiques*, 1939 and 1952). In thc samc spirit T., J. & J. Mayer registered in 1850 a well-known jug of rusticated tankard form with a relief depicting a boy birdsnesting (Fig. 1). One of the jugs being sold by Cork & Edge in 1855 was the "Cup Tosser" with a fortune-telling scene; another was a rusticated jug with a "Babes in the Wood" motif treated in a contemporary manner (Figs. 2 and 3) which was also apparently made by Alcock. In the later 'fifties, however, the fashion for all these heavily decorated styles was beginning to fade, and one of the last of the genre subjects was an irregular tankard-shaped jug decorated with farming scenes and sheaves of corn which was registered by E. & W. Walley in 1858.

Relief-decorated jugs of a commemorative nature were rather few in number, and they naturally covered a wide variety of subject-matter. In the broadest sense Henry Townsend's "Coach and Railway" jug may be considered commemorative, although the contrast which it points between stage-coach and railway travel does not seem to be associated with any particular person or occasion (Plate 21). Like the "Hop jug", this was commissioned by Henry Cole to be made by Mintons for his "Summerly's Art Manufactures" (see above). Equally well known is the curious Distin jug, apparently made both by Samuel Alcock and by Cork & Edge, which celebrates in a row of three-quarter length portraits the performance in the Potteries of the popular Distin family of instrumentalists (Fig. 2); similarly, popular interest (in A. H. Layard's Assyrian excavations) was expressed in a Ridgway & Abington jug of 1851, which was decorated with Assyrian motifs including the winged human-headed bull. Other more obvious occasions for commemorative jugs were provided by military events. The public concern in the Crimean war, which began in 1854, was expressed in a jug depicting military figures at home and abroad which was registered in January 1856 by James Pankhurst; and relief at the ending of the Indian Mutiny in 1857 was the occasion for a jug registered in 1858 by Cockson & Harding with a bust of General Havelock, and perhaps also the occasion for the Benjamin Green jug of the same year with a bust of Queen Victoria and Prince Albert. The unexpected death of Prince Albert in December 1861 resulted in the registration of three jugs in the following year, each of which was decorated with his bust. These were by the Old Hall Earthenware Company, J. Furnival and Thomas Cooper. In 1867 William Brownfield issued a commemorative jug dedicated apparently to the Emperor Napoleon III and presumably inspired by the great Paris exhibition of that year (Fig. 5); and in 1876 Wedgwood's tried the

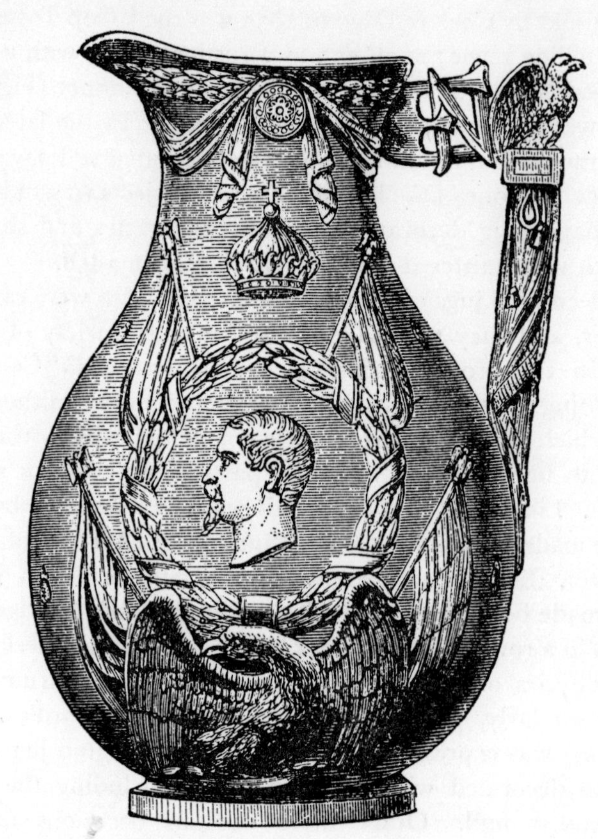

FIG. 5. Jug by W. Brownfield (*Art Journal* catalogue of the Paris Exhibition of 1867).

American market with a Centennial jug decorated with busts of Washington and Lincoln.

All the jugs described so far have been decorated with representations of human beings or of animals. These are, no doubt, the most striking to collect, but a serious interest in the design of the period should include the plant patterns, and formal motifs which equally represented aspects of contemporary taste, and which were also in many instances remarkably attractive.

The relief-decorated jugs of the late 'forties and early 'fifties represent better than any other ceramic medium a distinctive style of loose-running plant patterns. The style is to be contrasted with the isolated bunching of flower-sprays which had been characteristic of the revived rococo porcelain of the 'thirties and early 'forties; it was to be contrasted also with the somewhat austere sense of formality which was later to prevail in the 'sixties, and with the slight isolated sprays which were often used in a Japanese manner in the 'seventies

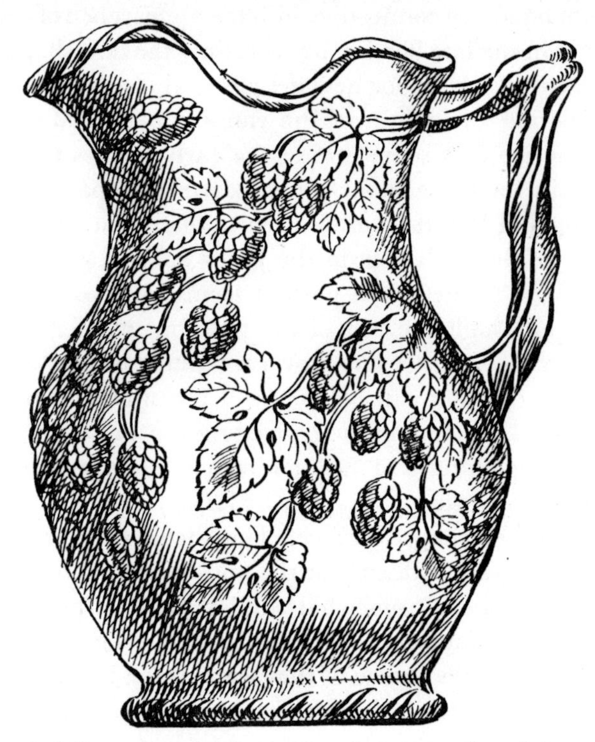

FIG. 6. Minton jug, registered in 1848 (reproduced from the records of the Patent Office Design Registry).

and 'eighties. In the running patterns of the mid-century years the plants were disposed in an entirely free and naturalistic manner over the surface to be decorated: often the handle of a jug would be represented as a stem of the decorative plant which would appear to grow out from the handle over the surface of the vessel; or, in the case of hop or vine motifs, the plant stems might cling to a rusticated handle (Fig. 6).

The sense of undisciplined naturalism was heightened in many instances by giving the outline of the jug the irregularity of tree growth and the surface texture of bark, so that the whole appeared as a tree stump around which is growing the appropriate foliage (Plate 22). Alternatively the plant decoration around the stump might be a climbing plant, such as a convolvulus, as in the case of the well-known T., J. & J. Mayer jug which was illustrated in the *Art Journal* catalogue of the 1851 Exhibition (Plate 23). For the purpose of simulating a stump a jug needed to be roughly straight-sided; this fact may not have any connection with the appearance of the tankard shape of jugs in the late 'forties, but certainly the new shape was used immediately as the basis for new designs of this nature.

In considering the origin of the running plant patterns it is of interest to notice that some jugs of the early 'forties with coloured plant patterns have the plant sprays scattered separately over the surface instead of joined together to form one plant. An instance of this manner of design is seen in the Jones & Walley jug of 1843 on Plate 24. Here a relief plant pattern seems to have sprouted from the handle, although the rest of the pattern, transfer printed and tinted by hand, consists of an all-over treatment of separated sprays. Perhaps this treatment can be seen as a transitional stage between the bunches and garlands of the revived rococo and the continuously disposed running patterns of the later 'forties, but it must be admitted that the use of separated sprays may be largely dictated by the use of transfer prints on a shaped surface. The Victorian running patterns seem to appear quite suddenly in the mid-'forties, and may be connected with the use of somewhat similar patterns in relief on the French Beauvais stoneware. The term "running patterns" was, incidentally, used in a review of that ware at the Paris Exhibition of 1844, which appeared in the *Art Union* magazine during that year.

These patterns are naturally seen at their best when they form the sole decoration of a vessel, but they also appear as a detail to give an authentic mid-century touch to many of the jugs depicting figures and scenes. The gothic jugs were excluded; not even Victorian fantasy could marry these sprawling plants with the formalities of gothic masonry. But many of the genre jugs, and jugs with classical figures, offered an excellent opportunity for the incidental use of plant motifs growing from the handle and for the use of the tankard shape, and similar shapes, in the form of a tree stump (Fig. 1). The jugs with classical figures were mostly adorned with vines disposed in this distinctively loose and un-classical manner; and the Minton example in Plate 19 has an irregular, slightly bulbous shape which seems to have been suggested by a vine stock.

Another style of plant pattern, conceived in a similarly realistic spirit, consisted of a plant growing vertically up the side of a vessel from the base. This treatment naturally had the effect of producing a pattern of dense growth at the base, thinning to an almost undecorated band at the top. Probably the first of the jugs to be decorated with a relief pattern of this sort was a Ridgway & Abington jug with a pattern of bulrushes which was registered in 1848. This

FIG. 7. Jug by Ridgway & Abington (*Journal of Design and Manufactures*, 1849).

was illustrated in the *Journal of Design and Manufactures* in 1849 (Fig. 7), where a commentator remarked that the design was derived from one by Richard Redgrave for Henry Cole's "Summerly's Art Manufactures" and that Redgrave's design had been unconsciously influenced by a Beauvais stoneware vase decorated with bulrushes. Richard Redgrave was a well-known painter whose design had been produced for Henry Cole in 1847; it depicted water plants and, painted on the side of a glass water jug or water carafe, it was intended to be "suggestive" of the vessel's contents. The idea was copied in many forms on pottery, porcelain and glass; among the designs for jugs one particularly attractive version is the "Tulip jug" which was registered by Copelands in 1856.

Another aspect of the same interest in naturalistic plant motifs was the use of vegetable forms for the whole shape of a vessel. This usage was also noticeable among the majolica and other wares of the period (see page 83), and was equally a feature of mid-Victorian silver. Jugs made in the form of logs have already been discussed since they are especially associated with the running patterns of leaves and twigs and of climbing plants; but many other vegetable forms are to be found spread over a very long period. Samuel Alcock registered in 1847 a jug which at first sight seems to be a log form, but on closer scrutiny turns out to be a bundle of sticks tied about the middle with a withy from which sprout a few leaves. Jugs are often found which purport to be formed wholly by the leaves of plants. This concept was especially popular about the middle of the century and in the 'fifties. Two typical examples are a Copeland jug of 1849, which has its whole surface figured to represent a lily-of-the-valley plant, and a Samuel Alcock jug of 1858, which is formed as though made of leaves and bulrushes. The idea was extended to include the fruit of a plant in a Minton jug of 1858 which appeared in the shape of a pineapple; this was followed in 1860 by a jug of Bates & Co. in the shape of a pine-cone, and 1864 by a jug of Brown-Westhead, Moore & Co. in the shape of a corn-cob. Another Minton example of 1875 was shaped as a large acorn standing upon a number of little acorns for feet. But the possibilities in this style were by no means limited to the representation of living vegetable forms. Many jugs of the 'fifties, 'sixties and 'seventies were given a surface to represent basketwork or wood. A jug registered by William Brownfield in 1855 is a relatively early example of the use of a basketwork surface; Wedgwoods registered a "Wicker jug" in 1880; Copelands used the effect of wooden staves in a jug of 1854; and R. G. Scrivener produced a jug in 1872 wholly in the shape of a wooden barrel. Perhaps the extreme of imitated forms was a jug registered in 1875 by the firm of George Jones, which was shaped to represent a swallow's nest with the bird itself peeping in to form the handle.

Alongside these exotic jugs, which developed from the mid-century sense of realism, the 'sixties saw the development of a novel style of restrained and formal decoration. Among the designs of this decade and the following few years, one finds repeatedly jugs with simple, formalised patterns in shallow relief. The patterns were derived from a wide variety of historical sources; but the treatment of the patterns was strikingly uniform. The ground of the patterns, and sometimes the reliefs themselves,were covered with a stippling of fine raised dots, the purpose of which was no doubt to cover the imperfections which might appear on the smooth areas of a cast surface (Fig. 8). A parallel to this strain of comparative austerity in the

FIG. 8. Jug by Powell & Bishop, registered in 1872 (from a photograph in the Patent Office Design Registry).

'sixties and early 'seventies might be found in the popularity of plain engraved glassware during the same period. From about the middle of the 'seventies, on the other hand, the most remarkable feature of the new designs was the influx of ideas derived from the new interest in Japan (Fig. 9). Henceforth Japanese influence was to be seen in almost all categories of ceramic wares, in the use of random shapes and above all in the sprays of randomly disposed plant patterns, which were to culminate in the sinuously vertical "Art Nouveau" patterns of the end of the century.

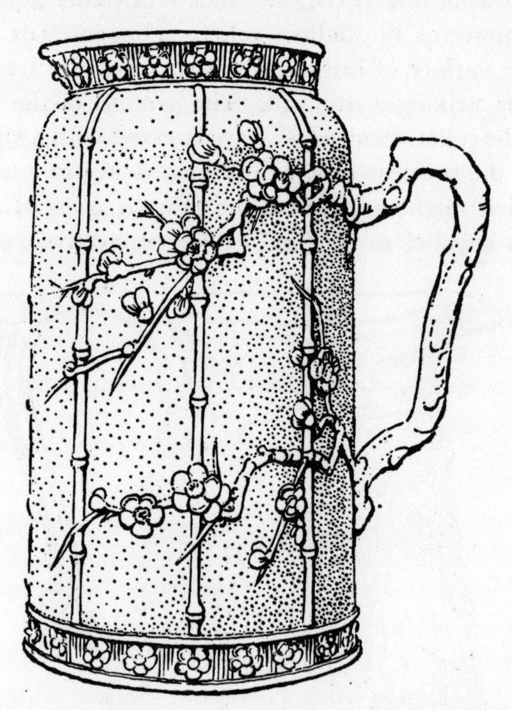

Fig. 9. Jug with "Japanese" sprays, registered by Pinder, Bourne & Co. in 1877 (from a photograph in the Patent Office Design Registry).

CHAPTER 3

POTTERY FIGURES

THE different potentialities of pottery or earthenware on the one hand, and of porcelain on the other hand, are nowhere better illustrated than in the art of figure-making. The fine nature of porcelain lends itself to extreme realism and to the use of expensive decorative details, whereas earthenware is more suitably made in forms which are the least exacting in moulds and decoration. In the second half of the eighteenth century the making of pottery figures was dominated and largely inspired by the novelty of porcelain, which was then being made in this country for the first time. In some degree the same circumstances applied in the earlier decades of the nineteenth century; but by Victorian times the artists and potters concerned with pottery figures had finally shaken off the influence of porcelain and were making simple, engaging wares for a popular and widely based market.

In the two or three decades immediately preceding Victoria's reign two main varieties of pottery figures were being made in Staffordshire, and to some extent these styles continued into early Victorian times. The first was primarily associated with John Walton about the eighteen-twenties, and is usually to be distinguished by the representation of bushes or trees, known as "bocage", as a background for the figures. The same style was used by Ralph Salt, whose work covered a slightly later period than that of Walton, and probably continued into the early 'forties; he worked in procelain as well as earthenware and used lustre decoration as well as enamel colours. The second variety of pottery figures belonging to this period is thought to be the work of Obadiah Sherratt. It consists of figure groups mounted on curious bracket feet. Bull-baiting is perhaps the commonest subject, but moral subjects also occur; and it may be noticed that one of the latter, using the new word "teetotal" in its title, must for that reason be dated well into the 'thirties (R. G. Haggar, *Apollo*, L, 1949).

A number of other pre-Victorian styles of figure work should be mentioned in this context, since they survived in common production into Victorian times. The toby jug, which was well established in the second half of the eighteenth century, continued as a favourite throughout the nineteenth century and beyond. Of a narrower span were the figure-shaped flasks, which were usually made of brown saltglazed stoneware or of earthenware with a brown "Rockingham" glaze (see page 160). The heyday of such flasks was during the agitation which led up to the Reform Act of 1832, when innumerable flasks were made to represent such personalities as Lord Brougham and Lord John Russell. The fashion for them did not last long, but they included some early Victorian personalities; one example shown here is made of white stoneware to represent the young Queen Victoria (Plate 25).

The English regard for domestic animals is demonstrated in the vogue for earthenware dogs as chimneypiece decoration, which lasted throughout the century. They are rarely marked, and they have about them a timeless quality which defies any but the broadest dating. The larger ones with a smooth outline were clearly designed to be made rapidly in the fewest possible moulds; and like the flat-back human figures, which will be discussed later, they are most typically the product of the mid-century years, although an individual example might have been made at almost any time subsequently. Smaller dogs, and some which are moulded and modelled in realistic detail, are likely to be earlier than the middle of the century. One characteristic trick of construction or decoration is of interest, since it provides a link with other decorative earthenware: patches of "fur" were formed of shredded clay which had been passed through a close mesh. The name "Rockingham" is often associated with this feature, but no doubt the great majority of these dogs were made in the factories of Staffordshire. It may be worth mentioning that these so-called china dogs are made of earthenware, and are not usually made of china in the sense of porcelain.

Obviously related to the furry dogs are the chimneypiece cottages and castles, decked with patches of vegetation formed in precisely the same manner of shredded clay. These toy buildings, with or without the vegetation, were being made in the greatest quantities about the eighteen-twenties, when they were designed as pastille-burners. A pungent pastille was burned inside, and the smoke emerged in realistic fashion from a chimney. The need for pastille-burning is said to have diminished with the notable Victorian advance in sanitation, and the toy buildings survived merely as chimneypiece ornaments, to be chosen as an alternative to human or dog figures. The earlier ones are anonymous, but in the mid-century period they were often given titles to commemorate a Crimean War victory, a famous crime or a residence of royalty.

The making of pottery figures was a continuing art-form, and it is all the more surprising, therefore, that in human representation a strikingly new, and technically retrograde, style of figures should have appeared in the early years of Victoria's reign. The strange feature of the new figures was the fact, which has already been remarked, that they were even less like porcelain figures than their predecessors; and this was so in an age of increasing realism and mechanical exactness. A parallel may be found in the naïveté of the Victorian glass "friggers" or toys, and in the similar peasant-art quality of many varieties of popular prints. It may be that the Victorian figures were the first entirely decorative wares to reach in quantity the simplest homes of the countryside and the towns, and to that extent they may have fulfilled a different function from that of their forerunners. Certainly their simplicity of design and colouring gives them an especial charm for us today, and they have long been a subject of great interest to collectors.

The commonest variety of Victorian pottery figures is commonly called the flat-back. This was so named because the figure was designed to be seen only from one side, and was flatly formed with little modelling or colour on the rear surface. The figure was designed entirely as a chimneypiece ornament and its effect was essentially two-dimensional (Plate 26). As such, it needed fewer moulds than a wholly three-dimensional model and was consequently cheaper to make. Most of the flat-backs were made by pressing in a simple two-piece mould, with only an occasional subsidiary mould, to form perhaps the front leg of a prancing horse. The process of casting in a slip mould was only rarely used for these figures, presumably because slip moulds needed replacing more often than press moulds; this can be taken as a further indication that these figures were intended for the cheapest market, since even such popular wares as the relief-decorated jugs were nearly always made at this period by the more effective method of slip casting.

The flat-backs were made during the whole of the second half of the nineteenth century. The most flourishing period, when presumably the greatest numbers were made, was during the 'fifties and early 'sixties. After a decline in the later 'sixties and some revival in the 'seventies, the art was slowly dying towards the later years of Victoria's reign. The evidence for this cycle is derived from an analysis of the figures which are intended as portraits of individual celebrities or are obviously associated with historical events. It should be remembered, however, that by no means all the figures bore titles or can for other reasons be placed in these categories.

It is certain that the flat-back figures are closely associated with the firm of Sampson Smith of Longton, who was working in Longton from the later 'forties until his death in 1878. This firm continued into the later nineteenth century, and even today the name is used by a modern firm. Only a very few marked figures are known, but these nearly all bear Sampson Smith's name. In 1948 some fifty or so of the old press moulds were found by the present firm, including many flat-back figures, as well as dogs and cottages. We must presume that Sampson Smith dominated the market, but there must also have been many other small manufacturers, some of them very small indeed, who would be prepared to follow Sampson Smith's lead in the production of the simplest sort of figures. Many of them must be included among the names in the long list of such manufacturers compiled by R. C. Haggar and published in his *Staffordshire Chimney Ornaments* (1955), and certainly many flat-backs and similar figures were also made in Scotland in potteries such as those at Prestonpans and Portobello (Plate 27).

Besides the flat-backs, two distinct varieties of fully-modelled Victorian figures are presumed to have been made in Staffordshire. Thomas Balston, in his *Staffordshire Portrait Figures of the Victorian Age* (1958), discusses two groups which he considers to be the work of two unidentified firms, and which he proposes to name "Alpha" and "Tallis". The Alpha figures are carefully and elaborately modelled in the porcelain tradition (Plate 29). They include, besides historical figures, representations of contemporaries such as the singer Jenny Lind and the dress reformer Mrs. Bloomer, which point to a period of manufacture about the later 'forties. The identification of the Tallis figures centres around a group of theatrical figures based on illustrations in Tallis's *Shakespeare Gallery*, which was published in 1852–3.

19. White stoneware jug with 'Silenus' group on a blue coloured ground; about 1840–45. On the base is a raised cartouche inscribed 'No. 235' and 'M' (Minton). Ht. $7\frac{5}{8}$ in. *Victoria & Albert Museum.*

20. The 'Hop jug', designed by Henry J. Townsend. Originally commissioned by Henry Cole for his 'Summerly's Art Manufactures' and registered by Mintons in 1847, this version with coloured glazes (Palissy ware) was made in the later 'fifties. Ht. $10\frac{1}{2}$ in. *Victoria & Albert Museum.*

21

The 'Coach and Railway' (or 'Two Drivers') jug, designed by Henry J. Townsend; made by Mintons, originally for Henry Cole's 'Summerly's Art Manufactures' about 1847. On the base is a cartouche inscribed 'No. 335' and the initial 'M'. Ht. 7 in. *Victoria and Albert Museum.*

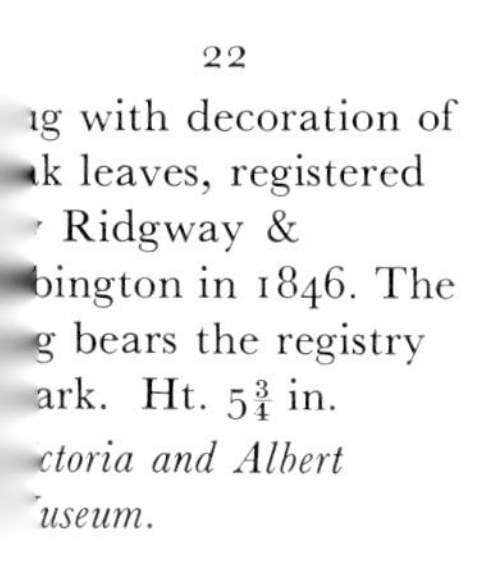

22

ıg with decoration of ık leaves, registered · Ridgway & bington in 1846. The g bears the registry ark. Ht. $5\frac{3}{4}$ in. *ctoria and Albert 'useum.*

23. Jug of brown ware with convolvulus decoration; the rim was originally fitted with a metal lid. The pattern was registered by T., J. & J. Mayer in 1850 and was illustrated in the Art Journal catalogue of the 1851 Exhibition. Ht. $7\frac{3}{4}$ in. *City Museum, Sheffield.*

Page 64

24

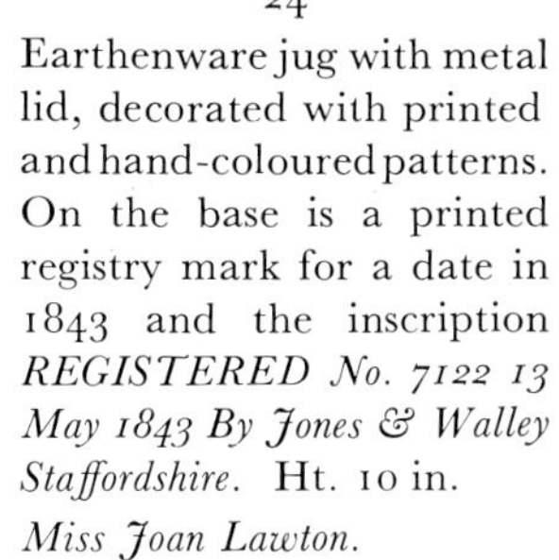
Earthenware jug with metal lid, decorated with printed and hand-coloured patterns. On the base is a printed registry mark for a date in 1843 and the inscription *REGISTERED No. 7122 13 May 1843 By Jones & Walley Staffordshire.* Ht. 10 in.
Miss Joan Lawton.

25
hite stoneware flask in the
'm of the young Queen
ctoria, inscribed on the base
ublished by S. Green, Lambeth,
July 1837'. Ht. 11½ in.
ctoria and Albert Museum.

26
Flat-back figure of Dick Turpin, probably modelled about 1850. Ht. $11\frac{1}{2}$ in.
Victoria & Albert Museum.

27
Group of two fishwives, made at the Prestonpans pottery; mid-nineteenth century. Ht. $9\frac{1}{4}$ in.
Royal Scottish Museum.

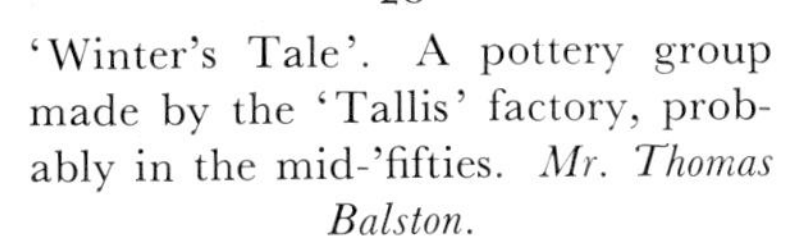
28

'Winter's Tale'. A pottery group made by the 'Tallis' factory, probably in the mid-'fifties. *Mr. Thomas Balston.*

29

Figures of Sir John Franklin (the well-known explorer) and Lady Franklin, made by the 'Alpha' factory, probably in the late 'forties. *Mr. Thomas Balston.*

30. Figures in Highland dress. A simple flat-back group, probably made in the 'fifties. Ht. 7 in.
Victoria and Albert Museum.

These are also fully modelled in the round, but are distinguished from the Alpha figures by various details of style, body material and titling (Plate 28). The group includes many other figures besides the theatrical characters, and the range of portrait figures runs from the young Prince of Wales in the late 'forties to General Gordon in the 'eighties.

In the eighteenth century many of the pottery figures had been decorated with coloured glazes. In Victorian times, however, this method of colouring was never used on the equivalent style of popular figures. Some ceramic figures were, indeed, covered with the coloured Majolica and Palissy glazes, but these were altogether more sophisticated and academically sculptural, and they were mainly the concern of the big factories (see page 93 and Plates 35 and 36). On the popular figures all the colouring was either under or over the glaze, and usually both processes were employed on the same figure. The underglaze colour was the more lasting and lustrous, since it was protected by the overlying glaze. It needed, however, to retain its colour through the heat of the glazing; in practice only two underglaze colours were used on the figures, blue and black. The underglaze black seems to have been a little difficult to control, but it was used, albeit sparingly, throughout most of the Victorian period. The material for the underglaze blue, which was derived from cobalt, had become relatively cheap at the beginning of the period, and a lavish use of this vivid colour is a striking feature of most of the figures of the 'forties and 'fifties. This applied particularly to the early flat-backs and to the figures of the "Alpha" factory, but it is interesting to notice that the figures of the "Tallis" factory do not have any underglaze colouring.

The overglaze colours were the sort known as enamels. They could be used for almost any shade of colouring, including an alternative to the underglaze blue and black. The variety of colours was due to the fact that although the enamel colours needed to be fired into the glaze they did not need to withstand nearly the temperature of underglaze colours. The disadvantage of overglaze colours was that they were somewhat dull and lacking in lustre for use over large areas and, unless they were very accurately fired, they tended to flake away. Gilding was carried out in the same manner as enamel colouring; that is, it was applied over the glaze and then subsequently fired into the surface of it.

During the heyday of the pottery figures, around the middle of the century, colouring was used extensively, although some proportion of figures were always left with only slight colouring. In the 'sixties the taste for colour seems to have receded. The underglaze blue in particular, which had been so characteristic of the figures made around 1850, seems scarcely to have been used at all after the early 'sixties. Many of the figures were now left largely in the white of the glazed body with only a few relieving touches of colour to distinctive features of the face and costume. Overglaze colours and underglaze black were, however, still used on occasions to colour large areas, and it would be misleading to insist too closely upon dating by the presence or absence of colour. Portrait figures can be found, which are largely coloured and yet from their subject-matter can only be dated to the later decades of the century; such were the figures of the American religious revivalists Moody and Sankey, who were not known in this country until the 'seventies.

The great majority of the figures, and especially the simpler and cheaper ones, were untitled and are to be regarded as purely decorative pieces. Their variety is immense and little work has been done in charting their subject-matter apart from those intended as portraits. Specialised collections of particular themes are therefore easy to form and are likely to be of great value to future research. Even the most naïve of figures must reflect in some degree the interests and tastes of those who bought them; they take us back in effect not only to popular Victorian styles and patterns but also to the popular sentiments of the period. The many versions of Uncle Tom and Eva, of *Uncle Tom's Cabin* fame, reflect again the anti-slavery agitation; and the numerous groups of figures in Highland dress are surely symptomatic of the romantic interest of the mid-century in the Highlands of Scotland (Plate 30).

The portrait figures, on the other hand, have been well explored. These usually have the name of their subject inscribed on the base and their features are portrayed in a recognisable manner. They have been carefully catalogued in Thomas Balston's *Staffordshire Portrait Figures of the Victorian Age*, where nearly two hundred subjects are listed and described. The great majority of the portrait figures represent contemporaries and most of these attracted popular interest at some specific time during the period. Many of them can thus be dated from the popularity of their names to within a very few years. An important group, for instance, consists of personalities connected with the Crimean War and must therefore have been modelled during the years 1854–6 or very shortly afterwards. Similar groups are connected with other warlike events which aroused popular sentiments in this country, such as the Indian Mutiny of 1957–9 and the Franco-Prussian war of 1870. Models of personalities connected with famous crimes, and models of their houses, can also be dated very precisely. On the other hand politicians, preachers, sportsmen and stage stars were likely to retain their popularity for a longer time. Many of the representations of the Queen and other members of the royal family were obviously made over a long period; but some of these, too, can be connected with precise events such as an 1854 group of the Queen with Napoleon III or an 1862 pair of the newly-wed Prince and Princess of Wales.

An interesting sidelight is thrown on the outlook of the modellers and their expected customers from an analysis of the preachers and politicians among the portrait figures. About eleven contemporary Nonconformist preachers are represented, compared with some four Roman Catholic personalities and only one slightly uncertain example of a Church of England clergyman. This disparity is matched among the politicians, where the Tory Benjamin Disraeli, the Earl of Beaconsfield, appears alone among some seven politicians of the left. There is no doubt that the market for the portrait figures was decidedly Nonconformist and Liberal (Thomas Balston, *ibid.*).

CHAPTER 4

JASPER, GRECIAN WARES AND TERRACOTTA

IT IS perhaps surprising that Victorian taste included a partiality for unglazed or slightly glazed wares. Just as the new Parian porcelain was left almost unglazed in order that it should resemble the marble of Classical statuary,* so the unglazed red and black pottery was justified by the red and black figured wares of classical antiquity. It may be, however, that the Victorian taste for unglazed pottery, and especially the red coloured sort, can also be thought of as part of a reaction against the fine finish and the artificiality of factory-made table-wares.

Jasper is a term applied to a peculiarly dense stoneware body, which can be used either in its plain white state or else with a deliberate coloration. Like the similar "black basaltes" body, it was originated by the great Josiah Wedgwood in the latter part of the eighteenth century and was subsequently associated mainly with the Wedgwood firm. For technical reasons the coloured jasper was normally used as a coating on a white jasper body, and this was known as "jasper dip"; the use of solid coloured jasper was, however, revived in 1856.

Jasper-ware was not glazed, and its decoration consisted typically of white jasper motifs, which were moulded separately and applied to a coloured jasper surface. The applied motifs were usually conceived in a classical spirit, and many of them were figure motifs designed for Josiah Wedgwood by such artists as John Flaxman, R.A. (b. 1755, d. 1826). Naturally jasper-ware was expensive; but as a luxury product it was remarkably successful in the late eighteenth and early nineteenth centuries, and some of the most attractive patterns have been in almost continuous production since that time, especially in the most characteristic combination of white relief decoration on a blue ground.

* See Companion Volume: Geoffrey Godden, *Victorian Porcelain*, 1961.

FIG. 10. "Etrurian" wares by Copeland & Garrett (*Art Union*, 1846).

The association of jasper-ware with classical ideas was very strong; but, in spite of this, Wedgwoods were slow to take advantage of the new wave of enthusiasm for classical forms which was developing during the first decade of Victoria's reign. The manufacture of jasper was at a low ebb and, although Flaxman's designs were respected, the old jasper-wares must by this time have appeared old-fashioned. In the years about 1847 there were several derogatory references to Wedgwoods in the *Art Union* magazine (later the *Art Journal*), and the firm was compared with Copelands which at that time was more active in producing classical wares (Fig. 10).

Just before the Great Exhibition, however, Wedgwoods began a revival of their jasper-wares, and at the exhibition itself jasper formed by far the most significant part of the firm's display (Fig. 11). "We rejoice", wrote the *Art Journal* commentator, "to see this eminent house again prepared to exert its position among the principal Art-manufacturers of the present day". Most of the designs were still based on the fine original creations of the eighteenth century. This was, no doubt, wise policy for the firm, but the resulting copies, or near copies, of eighteenth-century work are of little interest to

FIG. 11. Wedgwood jasper-ware at the 1851 Exhibition (*Art Journal* catalogue).

collectors. Of much greater interest and aesthetic significance are the less usual pieces of Victorian jasper which were designed wholly in the spirit of the mid-nineteenth century. The current use of plant motifs to form overall running patterns (see p. 51) was well suited to interpretation in jasper-ware. Some examples seem to have appeared at the 1851 Exhibition—an unidentified newspaper illustration in the Victoria and Albert Museum shows one instance—and several examples are shown in the *Art Journal* catalogue of the Paris Exhibition of 1855 (Fig. 12). Three vases which must be of this period are shown on Plate 31. Jasper-ware in this style does not seem to have been made later than about 1860, so that examples are not likely to be found with the factory date letters which began to be used in that year.

Although the original jasper-ware was classical in spirit, it was inspired less by classical pottery than by the Roman cameo-glass

FIG 12. Wedgwood jasper jug (*Art Journal* catalogue of the Paris Exhibition of 1855).

technique of the Portland vase (which is now in the British Museum). It was in his "black basaltes" body that Josiah Wedgwood set out to imitate in detail the admired red-figure pottery of classical antiquity; and in this he was followed by many other potters in the nineteenth century. Wares of this sort were usually called Etruscan or Etrurian, because they were largely known through finds in Italy; today the type is described as Greek, or more precisely as Attic red-figured ware of the fifth century B.C. The original ware was unglazed and, indeed, was made long before the regular use of glaze on pottery, so that imitations of it necessarily belong to the category of unglazed wares.

In the 'forties the revival of interest in classical forms led to a corresponding increase in the popularity of imitation Greek wares. In 1846 Copelands were being warmly complimented in the *Art Union* for their "Etrurian" ware in a dark material (Fig. 10). The firm of F. & R. Pratt of Fenton was making a similar ware and, in 1847, it produced an impressive piece "made of Staffordshire clays" which was no less than four feet high. Although too large to be a convincing imitation, the size of this *tour de force* attracted the attention that was intended (Fig. 13). "The adoption of these forms", wrote the reviewer in the *Art Union*, "is indeed, one of the most cheering signs of the times"; and in the following year, 1848, it was reported that Prince Albert had bought the vase, with a request for a companion piece.

Another firm whose mark appears often on jugs and urns of this character is Dillwyn & Co. of Swansea. An example of this ware, which seems to have been made from about 1848, is shown on Plate 32. Like most of the imitations—and like the originals—the red body has been painted in black around the motifs to leave the patterns and figures in red against a black ground. But the decorating firm which made perhaps the greatest speciality of this work—even to painting in the Greek style on Greek pottery forms made of glass—was that of Thomas Battam in London; and the apogee of the taste for the "Etruscan" wares may be seen in their display at the 1851 Exhibition which appeared as a cave packed with pots and meant to represent the inside of an Etruscan tomb (Fig. 14). The taste was perpetuated, however, during at least another decade. As late as 1861 a typical Greek-style vase from Battam was among the presentation pieces to be offered by the subscription club known as the "Crystal Palace Art Union."

FIG. 13. "Etruscan" vase by F. & R. Pratt (*Art Union*, 1847).

Fig. 14. Thomas Battam's "Etruscan tomb" at the 1851 Exhibition (*Art Journal* catalogue).

Unglazed red pottery of this sort might be regarded as terracotta, but generally this term was used for wares with moulded relief decoration. The Italian words *terra cotta* mean simply "burnt earth" or "earthenware" and were historically applied to Italian work of the Renaissance period. In the context of nineteenth-century pottery wares, terracotta can be described simply as a fine red earthenware, used without a glaze. Occasionally a very light-coloured terracotta might be defined as white terracotta, but the term as applied to pottery would not normally include colouring outside the range from red to buff or white, although it might include other colouring in its use for architectural purposes.

In the middle of the century the interest in terracotta as a ceramic material centred on its use for large objects such as garden vases and architectural features. French manufacturers were chiefly responsible for developing this use of the material, especially during the 'forties. In the later years of that decade, however, Willock & Co. of the Ladyshore works in Lancashire were often referred to for their

FIG. 15. Terracotta vase by Blanchard of Lambeth (*Art Journal* catalogue of the 1851 Exhibition).

architectural ornaments and similar large-scale work in terracotta. With the preparations for the 1851 Exhibition came a sudden flush of interest among English firms, ranging from established potteries, such as Mintons and F. &. R. Pratt, to firms which were to establish a specialist concern with large-scale terracotta, such as Blanchard of Lambeth (Fig. 15) and J. Pulham of Broxbourne. In 1858 Copelands were noted as showing two large terracottas, busts of Minerva and Juno, in the Ceramic Court of the Crystal Palace. In the Paris Exhibition of 1867 and the South Kensington Exhibition of 1871 the Lambeth firm of Doultons was represented by large terracottas and, among other works, a striking feature of the latter Exhibition was a terracotta fountain designed by John Sparkes and modelled by

George Tinworth, which was later erected in Kennington Park (see page 109).

Large-scale terracotta work had perhaps more connection with the techniques for using "artificial stone" or cement than with the normal processes of ceramic manufacture. The shapes of the garden vases in particular were usually classical or Renaissance, and they were conceived more in terms of stone sculpture than of clay modelling. On the other hand, some small-scale terracotta work was produced in the factories by artists whose approach was that of the modeller. Wallace Martin, the senior of the Martin brothers, was concerned with terracotta work in this manner during his short spell at the Fulham Pottery (see page 114); and George Tinworth of Doultons achieved most of his contemporary fame through his terracotta panels illustrating biblical scenes in high relief. In 1883 an exhibition devoted wholly to Tinworth's work was held in London and is the subject of a detailed review in the *Art Journal* of that year.

Besides its use for architectural and sculptural purposes terracotta was much used for small pottery wares in the latter part of the nineteenth century. It should be remembered that from the time of the Elers brothers in the seventeenth century unglazed red wares had been familiar in this country, usually with a highly fired body which is described as stoneware. The great Josiah Wedgwood made a well-known use of it in the ware which he called "rosso antico", and the same body seems to have been continued in the unglazed wares from the Wedgwood factory in the later nineteenth century. But most of the Victorian terracotta was merely the earthenware implied by its name, and the emphasis of its production was always upon its decorative qualities and its suitability for high-relief sculptural decoration. As such it differed from the earlier productions which were fired as stoneware in order to make them usable as table-wares.

The 1862 Exhibition included some remarkable small terracotta wares made by Wills Brothers of London in a purely decorative or sculptural style. The material in this case was quite soft, and it is significant that the designs were for casting in either terracotta or metal. An example is shown here of a tankard from this firm, which was illustrated in the *Art Journal* catalogue of the 1862 Exhibition (Plate 33). But the most outstanding of the small terracotta wares of the latter part of the century were those of the Watcombe company. Their works were founded in the late 'sixties on the site of a bed of fine clay a few miles from Torquay. Their products were first shown to a wide public at the South Kensington Exhibitions of 1871 and 1872, where they were commented on with enthusiasm. It will be noticed that these were the Exhibitions at which Doultons of Lambeth were attracting similar attention with their earthy sombre-coloured saltglazed ware (see Chapter 6), and the wide popularity of both wares can perhaps be seen partly as a reaction against the technical perfection of the more sophisticated factory productions.

The Watcombe terracottas included architectural features, figures, and even life-size busts and table-wares, besides such small decorative objects as table vases, candlesticks and jardinières. The warc was relatively hard and the relief decoration sharply defined. Some areas were often decorated with blue glaze, with black colouring or with

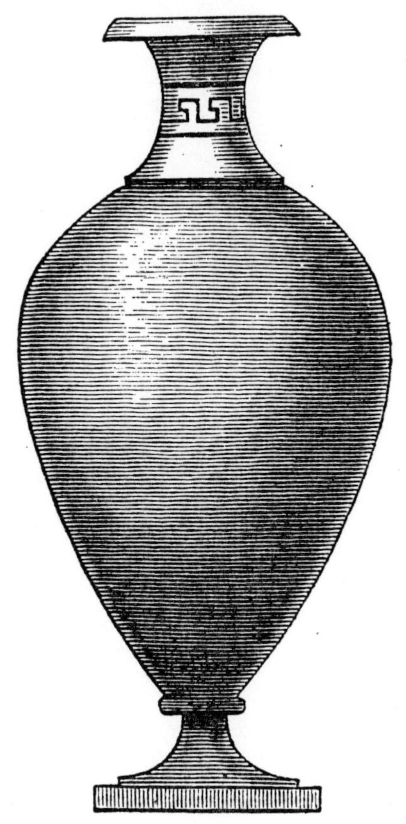

FIG. 16. Watcombe vase (*Art Journal* catalogue of the South Kensington Exhibition, 1872).

gilding, and sometimes relief decoration was carried in clay of a contrasting colour. Generally, however, both relief decoration and colouring were used sparingly, and large areas were left bare to emphasise the smooth beauty of the delicately coloured clay body (Plate 34 and Fig. 16). The shapes were cleanly proportioned, often with the high shoulders which were originally of classical inspiration. Most of the designs were presumably derived from a certain Charles Brock, who was brought from Hanley in the early stages of the firm to become manager and art director.

Very similar to the Watcombe wares were those of the Torquay Terracotta Company, which was founded in 1875 to work from a similar source of clay. The wares of the two firms are not, however, likely to be confused, since both are clearly marked on the base with their respective names.

CHAPTER 5

MAJOLICA, PALISSY AND HENRI DEUX

MAJOLICA was perhaps the most characteristic earthenware of the Victorian period and, if approached with discretion, it offers to the collector a wide field for research. Like many Victorian products its limits are ill-defined and some undoubted confusion is caused by the fact that the word "majolica" emerged from the nineteenth century into modern usage with a meaning which has little connection with its historical prototype. The original majolica, or maiolica, of the Italian Renaissance was an earthenware covered with an opaque white glaze; like the other historical earthenwares of this class, such as Dutch and English "delft" and French "faience", majolica was decorated by painting carried out on the raw glaze before it had been fired. On the other hand, Victorian majolica, and modern industrial majolica, are usually wares with a coloured glaze in which the interest is concentrated on the colour itself and on bold relief decoration. It is the material of the innumerable late-Victorian jardinières which were bought to house aspidistra flower-pots. It is also the material of many charming figures and figure groups of the 'fifties and 'sixties, often modelled in the large doll-like style which was admirably suited to a decoration of brightly coloured glazes (Plate 35). Green is particularly a glaze colour associated with this majolica, and the material naturally lent itself to the mid-century fashion for vegetable forms (see page 54). The majolica chestnut dish on Plate 37 is delightfully apt as an expression of mid-century taste, since it is modelled from vegetable forms which are themselves "suggestive" of the vessel's purpose.

Both of the objects mentioned so far were from the factory of Mintons in Stoke-on-Trent; and Mintons it was which started the Victorian craze for majolica, and which perhaps was responsible for misnaming it. It is said that Herbert Minton, the principal of the firm, was in France in 1849 and saw by chance in Rouen some

FIG. 17. Minton majolica vase (*Art Journal* catalogue of the 1851 Exhibition).

common flower-pots with a green opaque glaze. He had already a Frenchman at his factory, called Léon Arnoux, who was carrying out technical experiments; to him was entrusted the inception of a new style of pottery. There was scarcely anything new about the technique of the pottery which resulted, and precedent could be found for most of the styles of its modelling; and yet in its final effect the ware was thoroughly at one with its period and far more original than might be thought from the historical name with which it was tagged.

The first pieces of Minton majolica were ready in time for the 1851 Exhibition. One was illustrated in the *Art Journal* catalogue and is reproduced here (Fig. 17). The original, or a similar piece, has survived in the Victoria and Albert Museum; it is strangely coloured and modelled in heavy relief without any painted decoration. The first great display of Mintons' majolica was at the Paris Exhibition of 1855; and in 1856 an *Art Journal* commentator was remarking that "the Minton majolica is one of the most successful revivals of modern pottery". By the time of the 1862 Exhibition majolica of this sort was an established fashion; indeed, the Minton firm was even prepared to emphasise it to the point of producing for that Exhibition an

31
Jasper-ware vases of the 'fifties, made by Wedgwoods (marked). Ht. of lefthand piece 8 in. *City of Portsmouth Art Gallery Collections.*

32
An example of the 'Etruscan ware' made by Dillwyn of Swansea, about 1850. Ht. $14\frac{3}{8}$ in. *Victoria & Albert Museum.*

33. Terracotta vase and cover with relief decoration of Diana and Actaeon, made by Wills Brothers, London, and shown at the 1862 Exhibition. On the base is inscribed *Wills Bros., Scpts., London. Published as the Act directs, 1858.* Ht. $10\frac{1}{2}$ in. *Victoria & Albert Museum.*

34. Terracotta vase with applied relief decoration, areas of blue glaze and gilding; made by the Watcombe factory, Torquay, probably in the early 'seventies. On the base, printed in black, *WATCOMBE TORQUAY*. Ht. 14½ in. *Victoria & Albert Museum*.

35

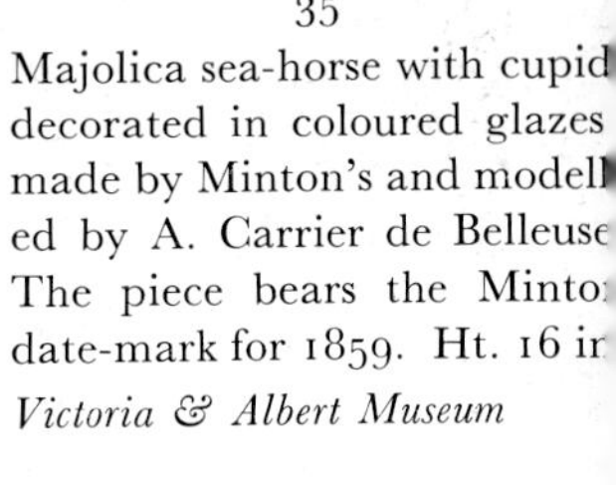
Majolica sea-horse with cupid decorated in coloured glazes made by Minton's and modelled by A. Carrier de Belleuse. The piece bears the Minton date-mark for 1859. Ht. 16 in. *Victoria & Albert Museum*

36

Figure of a cupid with a nautilus shell, decorated with coloured glazes and described as an imitation of Palissy ware; Minton date-mark for 1859. Ht. 9 in. *Victoria & Albert Museum.*

37. Majolica chestnut dish with matching spoon; made by Mintons and apparently bearing the factory date-mark for 1855. Ht. 5¾ in. *Victoria & Albert Museum.*

38
Green-glazed majolica plate, made by Wedgwoods about 1860; marked *WEDGWOOD* impressed. Diam. 8⅜ in. *Victoria & Albert Museum.*

39
Plate with moulded and countersunk decoration, the inner area covered with a green glaze and the border with a brown glaze. On the base is impressed *WEDGWOOD* and the factory date-mark for 1864. Diam. 6⅝ in. *Victoria & Albert Museum.*

40
Majolica tazza made by Mintons about 1858; the painted decoration is by Christian Henk. Length 8¼ in. *Victoria & Albert Museum.*

41
Majolica dish with a painting of a Roman soldier after Mantegna made by Minton's and shown at the 1862 Exhibition; on the base is the painted mark *MINTON*. Length 13 in. *Victoria & Albert Museum.*

42. Group of majolica pottery designed by Alfred Stevens for Mintons. All except the smaller vase have inscriptions on the base dated to 1864, but similar pieces seem to have been shown at the 1862 Exhibition. Ht. of the larger vase 17 in.

ambitiously designed majolica fountain. As developed for these purposes the Victorian majolica consisted of a cane-coloured body which might be glazed and coloured in a number of ways, according to the colour-scheme required, with opaque or clear glazes, placed directly on to the body or perhaps on to a white opaque ground.

The style of heavily modelled majolica called for the design of sculptors and, perhaps through the influence of Léon Arnoux, three French sculptors followed one another at Mintons during the 'fifties, modelling for majolica and parian porcelain. They were Emile Jeannest, Albert Carrier de Belleuse (Plate 35) and Hugues Protat, and all of them, besides working at Mintons, were teachers in the newly-founded Potteries' Schools of Design. The tradition of modelling for majolica continued at Mintons into the later decades and among the more attractive examples of the later work are the animal figures which were made by John Henk, the son of the Minton painter Christian Henk.

Two Staffordshire firms which made a particular use of majolica were George Jones and Adams & Co. The work of both is described in the *Art Journal* catalogue of the 1871 Exhibition. The phrase "for the million" was used of the Adams's output and there is no doubt that Victorian majolica had become popular in the fullest sense of the word. It is said that Wedgwoods began making majolica in 1860, and the firm began to revive their own late eighteenth-century production of green glazed plates moulded with an overall decoration of superimposed leaves (Plate 38). One feature, however, distinguished Wedgwoods' majolica from most of the rest: it was made on a white instead of a cane-coloured body, and presumably for this reason none of the glazes used on it were made opaque. An interesting extension of Wedgwoods' majolica was the use of a clear coloured glaze over a deeply impressed pattern to obtain an almost photographic effect from the varying depths of the glaze (Plate 39). This technique was no doubt derived from the similar *émaux ombrants* which had been first produced in the 'forties at the French Rubelles factory.

This is perhaps the place to mention the Wedgwood Rockingham wares. The word "Rockingham", as commonly used by industrial potters since the mid-nineteenth century, implies simply a ware with a manganese-brown glaze. Rockingham teapots and the like will be discussed elsewhere as part of the output of the smaller potteries (see page 160). The Wedgwood firm, however, was producing in the second half of the nineteenth century a sophisticated variety of Rockingham ware which was expensively decorated by wheel engraving or by acid etching. This unusual manner of decoration was carried out by the Stourbridge glass-decorating firm of J. & J. Northwood, and it was probably suggested by the fact that this firm was engaged in sharpening and polishing on the glass-engravers' wheels the jasper-ware reproductions of the Portland vase which were made in the late 'seventies.

Naturally some of the nineteenth-century majolica, having regard to its Renaissance prototype, was given painted decoration; and sometimes majolica was painted with Renaissance arabesques in a manner which certainly recalled the originals, although it does not seem normally to have been painted on the raw glaze in the manner which to modern eyes is an essential feature of the Renaissance work. A modest example of arabesque painting on an opaque glaze is shown on Plate 40. The painting on another Minton example, on Plate 41, is slightly appropriate to the extent that its subject was taken from an Italian Renaissance painting. More original work on a majolica glaze was carried out by Thomas Kirkby, a factory painter at Mintons who also worked on porcelain (see page 138 and Plate 77). But perhaps the most distinguished pottery which can reasonably be called painted majolica was a group designed by the well-known artist and designer Alfred Stevens, whose highly personal style was appropriately inspired by the motifs of the Italian Renaissance. These were apparently shown by Mintons at the 1862 Exhibition and some examples made a little later have survived in the Victoria and Albert Museum (Plate 42), but unfortunately they do not seem to have been made in any quantity.

The mid-century experiments with coloured glazes led the Minton artists to try their hand at imitating the work of the sixteenth-century French potter Bernard Palissy, who used coloured glazes to decorate his high-relief modelling. This was a period when Palissy's works were being rediscovered, and Minton's academic imitations of them attracted considerable attention. It is interesting to notice that the South Kensington Museum (now the Victoria and Albert Museum) acquired in 1860 an original Palissy ewer, a copy of which it had already acquired from Mintons in the previous year (Plate 43). But Mintons' "Palissy ware" was by no means confined to close imitations of the original style of Palissy. The description might be used for any ware with fine relief decoration and coloured glazes. For instance, when Henry J. Townsend's "Hop jug" appeared in a coloured glaze version in the later 'fifties, it was described merely for that reason as an imitation of Palissy ware (Plate 20 and see page 48). The adjectives "Palissy" and "majolica" were thus in some instances virtually interchangeable, and did not necessarily refer to anything more than a ceramic technique. The two similar sculptural pieces illustrated on Plates 35 and 36 were acquired by the South Kensington Museum on different occasions in the same year; they were recorded in the Museum as imitations of majolica and Palissy ware respectively; yet in neither instance is the style of modelling at all closely connected with the historical majolica or with the work of Bernard Palissy. It should be noticed that "Della Robbia" is another Renaissance term, used by Mintons at this time, which implies a similarity to majolica.

Most of the majolica or Palissy wares were relatively simple in nature and could be made with the ease and cheapness which is appropriate to earthenwares. In contrast the "Henri Deux" ware was exceedingly expensive and was embarked upon in a spirit of challenge. The historical ware which was known as Henri Deux or *Faïence d'Orion* in the nineteenth century is usually labelled today as Saint-Porchaire. Like Palissy ware, it was French; also, like Palissy ware, it belonged to the sixteenth century. It was difficult and expensive to make because its decoration consisted of coloured clays, reddish brown or chocolate brown, inlaid into a light buff-coloured body; such inlaid work involved considerable skills. The technique seems to have been first attempted in this country at Mintons in the later 'fifties under the watchful eye of Léon Arnoux, and many ambitious pieces appeared at the London Exhibitions of 1862 and 1871 (Plate 44). The best-known artist who worked in this medium at Mintons was Charles Toft, and it is recorded that in the early 'seventies a well-known piece from his hands, a combined barometer and thermometer case, was bought at great expense by Sir Richard Wallace, the founder of the Wallace Collection. Henri Deux ware was also made at other factories. Plate 46 shows a piece of the late 'fifties from Kerr & Binns of Worcester, although this is appropriate in style only and does not use the inlaid technique. At the Wedgwood factory the technique was explored over many years and it was often used for wares of an almost utilitarian character (Plate 45).

CHAPTER 6

DOULTONS OF LAMBETH

THE firm of Doultons was founded at Lambeth in 1815, and shortly became the partnership known as Doulton & Watts. Its business was the brown saltglazed stoneware which was being widely made at that time, and in the early years the factory was one of the main producers of the fancy flasks which were characteristic of the 'twenties and early 'thirties. To the early Victorians, however, saltglazed stoneware with its rough finish and mottled colour seemed crude and unsophisticated; the cheapest pottery could be white and pretend to be porcelain, just as the cheapest pressed glass could pretend to be cut crystal. As with many other simple popular wares, the decorative use of saltglazed stoneware faded away before the pretentiousness of the mid-nineteenth century. It survived only for utilitarian purposes, particularly for oven-ware, for large containers such as water filters and for ginger-beer bottles and drainpipes.

The revival of decorative saltglazed stoneware dates mainly from the group of wares which Doultons showed at the South Kensington Exhibitions of 1871 and 1872 (Fig. 18). At this time the head of the firm was Henry Doulton, who was later knighted. In the 'sixties he was on terms of friendship with John Sparkes, the headmaster of the nearby Lambeth School of Art, who later became the headmaster of the National Art Training School at South Kensington. Their interest in each other's affairs led to the novel experiment whereby a number of the pupils of the Lambeth School of Art, under the general direction of their headmaster, were given a free hand with the Lambeth pottery's saltglazed stoneware. The result was shown to the London public at the 1871 Exhibition and proved to be a style of pottery of great significance in the modern history of ceramics.

In many respects this ware can be said to mark the beginning in this country of the long process which was to lead to the development of modern studio pottery. It expressed some, at least, of the sentiments of the Arts and Crafts movement, and it may be regarded as

FIG. 18. Doultons' stoneware at the South Kensington Exhibition of 1872 (*Art Journal* catalogue).

the first important reaction in pottery against the effects of the industrial revolution. To the most discerning taste it was no longer automatically desirable that pottery should be mathematically exact in shape, a flawless white in colour or a reproduction of some other material. All of these technical goals, and many more, had been attained by the great factories of the mid-nineteenth century; but an original sense of clay, and of its capabilities and limitations, had been lost in the mechanical reproduction of technically excellent wares.

One of the first serious reviews of the new Lambeth ware was published in the *Art Journal* during 1874 by Professor T. C. Archer, the Director of the Museum of Science and Art in Edinburgh. In it he points the analogy between the new ware and the sixteenth- and seventeenth-century European stoneware whose makers were "guided by the nature of the material . . . and never played tricks with it by trying to make it do more than it was capable of being made to do well". Such theorising is very familiar to us today—far more familiar than the pottery which is being described, for in the meantime early Chinese pottery has been discovered and with it has come a wholesale change in the potters' source of inspiration. It is important to notice, however, that, although its prototype was openly acknowledged, the Lambeth ware was not in any sense imitative. The earlier European stoneware—usually called at that time *grès de Flandres*—had become very popular in the salerooms, but already the influence of the Far East was such that the angular shapes and impressed decoration of the European stoneware would scarcely have been considered suitable for direct imitation by students of art.

A practical advantage of saltglazed stoneware was that its firing was completed in one single operation. The relief decoration and the painting of the surface were carried out while the pot was still in the clay state; the thin, hard glaze was applied by the introduction of salt into the kiln at a certain stage during the single firing. This elemental simplicity not only satisfied a new sense of propriety in pottery, but also appealed to artists whose technical knowledge and experience of pottery-making were necessarily limited.

The Lambeth stoneware was naturally a highly self-conscious product. Those who made it, or at least those who decorated it, had the immediate intention of producing works of art rather than of selling for a market. But it is precisely this self-consciousness which gives the ware its historical importance and also its interest to the collector, for virtually all the pieces are signed by the artists responsible for the decoration and many of them are also dated (see Appendix VI). Every single piece has a scheme of decoration designed for itself alone, and always the decoration was carried out by the person who designed it. The modern potter did not, however, emerge in one sudden manifestation; it was to be another half century before the idea was fully developed of the artist potter who prepares and throws his own clay and who completes the process by firing his own pottery. At Doultons the decorating artists would have little concern with the composition of the clay body or the firing of it in the saltglaze kiln. These were clearly specialist matters; but it may be noticed that at Doultons, as at every other late nineteenth-century pottery, the crafts of throwing and turning, also, were separate mysteries to which artists did not aspire. In the studio a thrower and a turner were kept at work, and the decorating artists chose from their output the pots that they wished to decorate. In this way the decoration was designed and carried out on a pot to suit its shape and the known effect of a standardised saltglaze firing.

This was a considerable step forward, even though artist pottery was still far from the integration of potting processes which has since been achieved by modern studio potters.

It is said that at the Paris Exhibition of 1867 Doultons had shown some stoneware decorated with simple incised lines; and the ware shown at the 1871 Exhibition seems to have been predominantly decorated with sgraffito or incised patterning filled with colour. One of the first and best known of the Doulton artists, Hannah B. Barlow, consistently used this method for the main treatment of her stoneware pottery (see page 149). Her speciality was the representation of animals which she scratched on the smooth surface of the pots which she chose to decorate (Plate 47); and because of the nature of her decoration the pots she chose were ones with straight sides or else gently curving shapes. John Sparkes, in a lecture to the Society of Arts in 1874, described her style as possessing "a certain Japanese faculty of representing the largest amount of fact in the fewest lines". From a twentieth-century standpoint the one obvious criticism to be made of her work is that it does not display the economy of line that seems to be demanded by representational sketches on pottery. In this, as in many other aspects of Doulton pottery, and of late Victorian wares in general, one needs to evaluate style in terms of its own *milieu*, and to peer through the mists of "old-fashionedness" which inevitably enshroud the work of the recent past. Hannah Barlow's drawings are certainly spirited and well-placed on the ware they decorate. Usually they are scratched directly on to the body of the pot, and the scratching is emphasised by a filling of cobalt blue or other dark colouring. Sometimes a little modelling is given to the animal figures by touches of white; sometimes the figures are scratched through a white ground on to the body below. The decoration around the shoulders or necks of her pots, and perhaps around the bases, would consist of formal sgraffito patterning, painted and often also embellished with rows of white "beads". Such work used the resources which were common to the studio as a whole, and was carried out by assistants.

Hannah Barlow's sister, Florence E. Barlow, also decorated the stoneware on occasions with animals, especially with birds, painted in coloured clays. Most of the artists, however, who were working on the Lambeth stoneware during the early 'seventies were concentrating upon flat patterns of stylised foliage or seaweed. A third member of the Barlow family, Arthur B. Barlow, covered his pots with well-disposed flowing patterns of sgraffito work which were painted in the limited palette of colours available (Plate 48). Since the colours were under the glaze and needed to withstand the high temperature of stoneware firing, they were limited at first to shades of blue and brown, although other colours were to follow. White could be used in the form of a white clay, and this usually appears on the pottery in the form of an overall white slip or as the material for rows of beads and for little moulded bosses. Like the other male artists in the group, Arthur Barlow made a liberal use of the beads as a decorative device. At the time they had the attraction of a novelty when used on pottery of this sort; but today the pots with beaded decoration need a sympathetic eye, and even contemporaries were inclined to find the beading "a little overdone"; (these are in fact the words of a reviewer of a Doulton display in the *Art Journal* of 1874). Perhaps one of the attractions of the beading from the artist's viewpoint was that he had merely to indicate the line they were to take; the painstaking work of fixing them in position would then be carried out by assistants. This may perhaps also explain the awkward appearance of this style of decoration to eyes which are attuned to pottery made throughout by one artist; for the mathematically accurate little globules set in exactly drawn rows are scarcely at ease with freely drawn decoration.

Another woman artist who played an important part in the early years of the Doulton studio was Emily J. Edwards. A distinguishing feature of her decoration was the use of formal motifs, and especially the acanthus leaf, derived from classical Greek decoration. But many of her motifs consisted of freely drawn foliage, and she was fond of outlining them against a heavily patterned ground such as might be formed by a series of freely drawn vertical lines. Some of her unassuming work of this sort represents perhaps the most attractive pottery that ever came from this studio (Plate 49). Of the other men working in the studio, Frank A. Butler was a deaf and almost dumb artist who was often complimented by contemporaries for his originality in design. Certainly his designs covered a wide field of possibilities within the stoneware medium, and some of his work has considerable attraction, such as a bottle illustrated here with a strong overall repeat pattern (Plate 50). But the artist who was most praised of all was George Tinworth, and the reasons for the praise are by no

43
Ewer copied with some variations from an original example of Palissy ware; modelled by Hamlet Bourne, Stoke-on-Trent, and made by Mintons. The piece bears the factory date-mark for 1858. $10\frac{1}{2}$ in.
Victoria & Albert Museum.

44
Ewer of Henri Deux ware, with inlaid pattern of coloured clays; made by Mintons and shown at the 1862 Exhibition. On the base is the impressed mark *MINTON* and the date-mark for 1862. Ht. $15\frac{3}{4}$ in.
Victoria & Albert Museum.

45

Candlestick of Henri Deux ware, with inlaid decoration in black; made by Wedgwoods, probably in the early 'sixties. Mark *WEDGWOOD* impressed. Ht. $8\frac{1}{4}$ in.
Victoria & Albert Museum.

46

Covered tazza in the style of Henri Deux ware, with decoration painted in black; made by Kerr & Binns, Worcester, about 1859. Ht. $8\frac{1}{8}$ in.
Victoria & Albert Museum.

47. Doulton stoneware jug of 1874; the decoration, by Hannah B. Barlow, is incised on a white ground and filled with blue. On the base is an impressed mark *DOULTON LAMBETH 1874* and the incised monogram *HBB*. Ht. 6 in.
Victoria & Albert Museum.

48. Doulton stoneware jug of 1874; the decoration, by Arthur B. Barlow, is incised and painted in blue, grey and brown, with applied beads of white slip. On the base is an impressed mark *DOULTON LAMBETH 1874*, and the incised monogram *ABB*. Ht. $9\frac{3}{4}$ in. *Victoria & Albert Museum.*

Page 104

49. Doulton stoneware jug of 1871; the decoration, by Emily J. Edwards, is incised and partly coloured. On the base is an impressed mark DOULTON LAMBETH and the incised monogram *EJE*. Ht. $7\frac{3}{4}$ in. *Victoria & Albert Museum.*

50. Doulton stoneware vase decorated by Frank A. Butler, bought from the Philadelphia Exhibition of 1876. On the base is the incised monogram *FAB*. Ht. $9\frac{3}{8}$ in. *Victoria & Albert Museum.*

51. Doulton Faience vase painted by Mary Capes. Impressed *DOULTON LAMBETH FAIENCE* and date 1879, with painted monogram *MC*. Ht. $16\frac{1}{4}$ in. *Victoria & Albert Museum.*

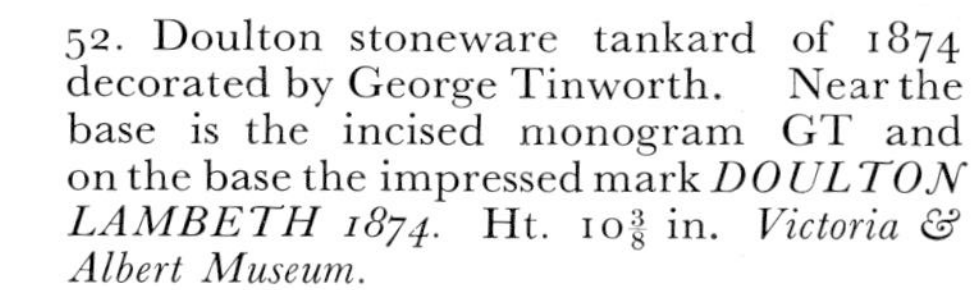

52. Doulton stoneware tankard of 1874 decorated by George Tinworth. Near the base is the incised monogram GT and on the base the impressed mark *DOULTON LAMBETH 1874*. Ht. $10\frac{3}{8}$ in. *Victoria & Albert Museum.*

53. Doulton Faience dish painted by Mary Butterton in 1876 and bought from the Philadelphia Exhibition of that year. On the base is the painted inscription *DOUTON & CO., LAMBETH* and the monogram *MB*. Length 14 in. *Victoria & Albert Museum.*

54. Doulton Silicon vase decorated by Edith D. Lupton in 1888. The brown stoneware is carved and perforated and is painted in blue, black, white and gold. The date is impressed on the base, together with the incised initials of the decorator and the impressed mark DOULTON LAMBETH SILICON. Ht. $13\frac{1}{8}$ in. *Victoria & Albert Museum.*

Page 108

means always easy to understand. He was the first of the artists from the Lambeth School of Art to be associated with Doultons in the late 'sixties, although at this time he was presumably concerned chiefly with the modelling of a terracotta fountain which had been designed by John Sparkes the headmaster of the School and was shown at the 1871 Exhibition (see page 79). It was on his modelling that his reputation was mainly based and, besides a number of large works, he made for Doultons many small terracotta panels depicting biblical scenes in high relief. His pottery decoration shows a somewhat tiresome repetition of spiral motifs emphasised by rows of beading, although the overall effect is often one of considerable vigour (Plate 52).

In the later 'seventies an important innovation was the use of the so-called *pâte-sur-pâte* method of decoration. This implied painting in a light-coloured clay slip upon the dark body in order to achieve a tonal pattern in relief. The use of this method was no doubt suggested by the well-known *pâte-sur-pâte* decoration which M. L. Solon was putting on Mintons' porcelain in the 'seventies; but this was not a process which could be adopted for stoneware without a good deal of experiment, since it was necessary to achieve a close physical similarity between the slip and the body. In the list of Doulton artists, given by John Sparkes in the course of two lectures to the Society of Arts (see Appendix VI), Eliza (or Elise) Simmance and Eliza S. Banks were mentioned as two artists who were making an important use of *pâte-sur-pâte* decoration in the years immediately before 1880.

The success of the Doulton stoneware pottery led the firm to try the same studio methods in the production of other sorts of pottery. Within a year or two of the important showing of the stoneware at the 1871 Exhibition, the Doulton studio was experimenting with "faience". Today the word "faience" is usually taken to imply pottery which has painted decoration on an opaque tin glaze. This, however, is not quite the definition given by John Sparkes in his lecture in 1880 to the Society of Arts. "Faience", he said, "is a convenient term for any sort of earthenware that is not white"; and then he added that, although it has no clear meaning, it "is a conventional term for painted pottery, on any ordinary natural clay as a body." As with the stoneware the effect of the faience was to stress a certain conscious regard for the materials in which the pottery

Fig. 19. "Impasto" vase by Doulton, Lambeth (*Journal of the Society of Arts*, 1880).

was made and decorated. It was, however, one degree less elementary in its conception and less revolutionary than the saltglazed stoneware, for it needed two firings: the first to fire the body; and the second to fire the painting and the overlying glaze. As the faience was earthenware, and not stoneware, the firings were naturally both at lower temperature; this may have led to the use of a wider variety of shapes, and it certainly implied that a much wider variety of colours could be used. For all of these reasons the Doulton faience seems to have less personality, and to have had less historical significance, than the Doulton stoneware. But it is also true that to many the Doulton faience is likely to be more immediately pleasing.

Closely related to the faience, Doultons' "impasto" ware was developed in the later 'seventies (Fig. 19). In this instance the painting was carried out, not on the biscuit-fired body, but on the raw clay of the unfired vessel, and thickened colour was used, which gave a slight relief to the pattern.

As with the stoneware, the decoration of the faience and "impasto" ware was carried out by school-trained artists, and their initials are normally to be found on the base of the pottery. At Appendix VI (a) (ii) will be found a list of the artists associated with these wares who were mentioned by John Sparkes in his lecture of 1880. Their styles of painting have very little in common, and embraced a wide assortment of subject-matter from landscapes and figures to simple geometrical and floral designs. The latter were probably the most attractive, and examples by two of the most competent of the artists, Mary Capes and Mary Butterton, are illustrated on Plates 51 and 53.

Another new ware was started in the early 'eighties called "Silicon". This was an unglazed brown stoneware, a little like the terracotta in appearance, but smoother and much harder. It was cut and carved, and "vases" were even made with perforated decoration (Plate 54); it was often decorated with inlays or *pâte-sur-pâte* work in clays of a contrasting colour, and gilding was used sparingly. But the attraction of the ware was clearly the texture of the natural fired surface and the decoration seems never to have been allowed to obscure more than a small part of it. A little later appear the first references to a third variety of Doulton stoneware, known as "Carrara". This was a dense white stoneware, with only a slight glaze, which gave its surface a texture suggestive of the marble to which its name refers. It was decorated with coloured patterns, often with a lustred effect. As with the Silicon ware, the most notable examples bear on their bases the initials of the artist who was individually responsible for their decoration; for instance, the example illustrated (Plate 55) bears the MVM of Mark V. Marshall, who was one of the best known of the Doulton artists around the end of the century.

There were other wares, too, such as "Chiné" and "Marqueterie", which are worth looking for (Plates 56 and 57). Chiné ware was decorated, often attractively, by the impress of lace on its surface. The body of Marqueterie ware was built up of a mosaic of coloured clays. In last years of the century, however, the saltglazed stoneware was still the most interesting of the Doulton productions. George Tinworth's work consisted mostly of sculptural modelling; but there were now several other artists at Doultons who were competent modellers and who often used saltglazed stoneware for their figures. Mark V. Marshall, who has already been mentioned, and F. C. Pope were both primarily modellers whose decoration on stoneware vases was inclined to take the form of naturalistic figures in full relief. Lizards and grotesques of various sorts are most frequently met with, but such motifs represented a taste which was characteristic of the period in general, and not merely of the Doulton artists. The revolutionary phase of innovation was now well past, but the artists associated with Doultons' studio in Lambeth continued almost alone to explore the potentialities of saltglazed stoneware for many years until the studio was finally closed with the movement of the factory in the nineteen-fifties.

It should be mentioned here that the name of Doulton is also associated with the branch factory of the firm which was established in the Potteries at Burslem in 1877. Earthenware was made there, but the reputation of the factory in Burslem was founded mainly on the production of fine porcelain in the later years of the century.

CHAPTER 7

THE MARTIN BROTHERS

THE revival of saltglazed stoneware by Doultons has been discussed in the previous chapter. Doultons' use of this particular pottery medium was undoubtedly successful by contemporary standards, and similar wares were produced by other factories with commercial saltglaze kilns in the London region, notably the Fulham Pottery and John Stiff & Sons of Lambeth. It was not, however, a medium that could easily be used by artist potters working alone on a small scale and, indeed, the only significant saltglazed stoneware made outside the factories in the nineteenth and early twentieth centuries was that of the Martin Brothers. Stoneware was considerably more difficult to produce on a small scale than earthenware and offered only limited opportunities for the use of colour; when eventually the rediscovery of early Chinese wares led to a new regard for stoneware, it was for stoneware with Chinese glazes and not with the saltglaze of European tradition.

The early history of the Martin brothers is complicated and somewhat confused, but if one is to appreciate their highly personal pottery it is necessary to bear in mind some of the factors which influenced their development. There were four brothers, all of them born in London, between 1843 and 1860. The eldest was Robert Wallace, then came Charles, Walter and the youngest, Edwin. Wallace was clearly the leader in the early days, and the association of the four in the making and selling of pottery was due mainly to his initiative.

As a result of early promise as a modeller Wallace spent several months of his youth in the studio of J. B. Philip, a sculptor with neo-gothic affinities. Later he was working as a sculptor's assistant on the carvings for the new Houses of Parliament, and this work was carried out among the casts of medieval carvings which had been assembled by A. W. N. Pugin for the edification of the stone-carvers. About 1860 he joined the evening classes of the newly-formed

Lambeth School of Art. Here he became a close friend of George Tinworth, who was later to become well known for his modelling at Doultons' Lambeth pottery (see pages 80 and 100). In 1864 both Wallace and George Tinworth were admitted to the Royal Academy Schools.

So far Wallace's ambitions were entirely those of a young sculptor. During most of the 'sixties he was an assistant in the studio of the sculptor Alexander Munro. His own private work appeared in the Royal Academy annual exhibitions of 1863, 1867, 1868, 1869 and 1872; and the example shown in 1869, a terracotta bas-relief called "The Woodland Spring" was thought sufficiently accomplished to be the subject of a whole page engraving in the *Art Journal* in 1875. His terracotta sculptures seem to have been mostly fired at Doultons' kilns, and it has been suggested that this experience may have turned his thoughts to pottery.

In 1871 he was working for a time at a pottery in Devon and then went to potteries in Staffordshire and elsewhere. In 1872 he was engaged as a modeller and designer, apparently of terracotta work, for the Fulham Pottery. This was the pottery at which John Dwight had made his stoneware in the seventeenth century. Its owner, C. J. C. Bailey, was anxious to revive its reputation for decorative wares, and in this he was no doubt moved by the developing success of Doultons' new stoneware. Accordingly he brought in Jean-Charles Cazin, a French painter and artist-potter who was in London at this period, to design decorative stoneware. Wallace Martin and Cazin were thus in direct contact at the Fulham Pottery, and both of them were experimenting in the possibilities of saltglazed ware. A piece of saltglazed stoneware decorated by Wallace about 1872 is in the Fulham Public Library, and one of Cazin's personal pieces of 1873 is illustrated in *The Connoisseur* of 1928. No doubt this contact played its part in Wallace's decision to begin making pottery on his own account. In 1873 he installed the whole of his parents' family in Pomona House in King's Road, Fulham, and proceeded to set up there a pottery studio and workshop for himself and his brothers.

Meanwhile Cazin, besides working at the Fulham Pottery, was teaching at the Lambeth School of Art. Before the move to Pomona House the two younger Martin brothers, Walter and Edwin, had been at the school, and seem to have been there about the time that

Cazin began teaching. In 1872–3 Walter, and then Edwin, had also been gaining some direct pottery experience as boy assistants in Doultons' studio. It was inevitable, therefore, that the wares made by Wallace with the help of his young brothers at Pomona House should be related both to the work of Cazin and to the new Doulton ware. A typical example of the earliest Martin stoneware is shown in Plate 58. It is marked "R. W. Martin, Fulham" and bears the date 1874. Its angular shape is decorated with carved, impressed and incised decoration, and it is sparingly coloured with cobalt blue and brown.

At first the firm was simply described as that of "R. W. Martin", and was concerned only with pottery decoration. Someone else had to throw the pottery, and it was fired in the Fulham kiln by an arrangement with C. J. C. Bailey. Walter was, however, learning fast to be a competent thrower and he soon took over this function. Already by 1874 Wallace felt sufficiently confident of the work to have it shown at the South Kensington Exhibition of that year; at the Exhibition, besides the pieces shown by Wallace, there was a fruit plate in stoneware which was described as the work of Walter. The *Art Journal* commentator remarked that the brothers were "trained in the same school with those who execute Messrs. Doulton's productions" and hence there was "a certain identity of thought . . . but it never takes the form of mere imitation, still less of any attempt at reproduction".

During 1874 the arrangement with Bailey came to an end, and for a few years the brothers fired their pottery in a glass crucible kiln which they hired at Shepherd's Bush. Finally, after much reconnoitring for a permanent site for a kiln and studio, they eventually found a suitable one beside a canal at Southall in Middlesex, and in 1877 they made the move there from Pomona House. When they worked in Fulham they marketed their wares by carrying them into the City, but after the move to Southall they felt the necessity of a shop in London, and about the beginning of 1879 a shop and gallery were opened in Brownlow Street off High Holborn. Henceforth the second brother, Charles, took charge of the shop and of most of the business arrangements; in effect he played the vital part of linking the brothers with their potential customers. Wallace, who continued to be the head of the firm, was concerned above all with modelling. Walter was the principal thrower, and also the kiln-burner and chemist. Edwin, who is said to have learned to incise pottery during his short youthful period at Doultons, was the principal decorator. But the association of the brothers was based upon more than a division of labour, and they did not by any means keep rigidly to precise roles: Walter often decorated pottery and Edwin did some of the throwing, especially of the smaller pots.

The four brothers were thus able to carry through by themselves virtually the whole process of pottery making and selling; for this reason they seem to us now to be closer than any other British potters of the nineteenth century to the modern conception of the artist-potter; but their self-sufficiency was probably due to practical rather than theoretical considerations. Certainly at one period they had some assistance, for in the late 'seventies Mark V. Marshall, later an outstanding modeller at Doultons, was with them as a boy; and his successor, W. E. Willey, carried out the decoration of a good deal of the ware produced in the years around 1890.

Within a few years of the pottery being established at Southall, Wallace began to include his own modelled figures among the Martin wares. By 1883 they were already attracting attention, and in that year a writer in the *Art Journal* referred to the grotesque birds and reptiles. The birds became characteristic Martin figures and Wallace continued to make them through almost the whole span of the pottery's existence (Plate 59). They belong to no known species of bird; their heads, forming covers for their hollow bodies, are loose and can be rotated; their faces are modelled with leering human expressions. They have a gothic quality, which is highly suggestive of popular medieval carvings; one can well imagine that they were derived from the impression made upon Wallace by Pugins' medieval casts among which he had worked as a youth. The same sense of the grotesque appeared later in the Martin jugs fashioned in the form of human faces, and in the wares decorated by incised drawings of fishes with comic facial expressions which were being made in the years around the end of the century. The taste expressed by work of this sort was by no means a peculiarity of the Martin brothers; it was a taste of the period, although to the mid-twentieth century it seems in some sense uncongenial. Not all of Wallace's models, however, appear in this light. A series of imps playing musical instruments are grotesques only in a mild and acceptable sense, and a number of small plaques and three-dimensional figures of a potter and his assistants are purely

55

Doulton Carrara jug decorated by Mark V. Marshall, probably about 1890. The decoration is formed partly in relief and is painted in grey-blue, purple lustre and gold. The initials of the decorator are incised on the base, together with the printed mark *DOULTON LAMBETH CARRARA*. Ht. 8½ in. *Victoria & Albert Museum.*

56

oulton Chiné vase of ne late nineteenth entury, decorated by ne impress of lace and y painting in enamel olours, purple lustre nd gold. Impressed ark *DOULTON & LATERS PATENT.* t. 7¼ in. *Victoria & lbert Museum.*

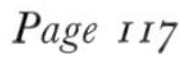

57

Doulton Marqueterie cup and saucer, about 1890. The body is formed of blue, buff and brown clays. Printed mark, inscribed "*12.7.87 DOULTON & RIX'S PATENT. MARQUETERIE.*" Diam. of saucer $4\frac{3}{4}$ in. *Victoria & Albert Museum.*

58

Stoneware jug, inscribed *R. W. Martin, Fulham,* with carved, impressed and incised decoration, partly coloured brown and blue. The jug is also inscribed with the number '2', and with the numbers '2 74' apparently for February 1874. Ht. $8\frac{1}{8}$ in. *Victoria & Albert Museum.*

59. Bird figure in stoneware with detachable head, modelled by Wallace Martin, coloured in browns and blues; inscribed *Martin Bros., London and Southall* and dated *11–1903*. Ht. $7\frac{1}{8}$ in. *Victoria & Albert Museum.*

Page 119

60. Figure of a thrower in stoneware, partly coloured, modelled by Wallace Martin; inscribed *RWM* (in monogram) *Southall, 12–1900* and *R. W. Martin & Bros., London & Southall*. Ht. $6\frac{7}{8}$ in. *Victoria & Albert Museum.*

Page 120

61
Stoneware vase (on wooden stand), with incised decoration on a brown coloured ground, inscribed *R. W. Martin & Bros., London & Southall* and dated *9–1886*. Ht. $9\frac{3}{8}$ in. *Victoria and Albert Museum.*

62
Stoneware vase with incised decoration on a brown coloured ground, made by the Martin Brothers about 1886; inscribed *R. W. Martin & Bros., London and Southall*. Ht. $8\frac{1}{2}$ in. *Victoria & Albert Museum.*

63
Stoneware vase with decoration incised and coloured in browns, black and green, inscribed *Martin Brothers, London & Southall* and dated *8–1890*. Ht. $3\frac{7}{8}$ in. *Victoria & Albert Museum.*

64
Stoneware vase with relief carved and incised decoration, coloured in browns and some blue, inscribed *R. W. Martin & Bros., London & Southall* and dated *2–1887*. Ht. 8 in. *Victoria & Albert Museum.*

65
Stoneware vase with decoration incised and coloured mainly in greens, greys and blues, inscribed *Martin Bros., London & Southall* and dated 5-1899. Ht. $10\frac{3}{4}$ in. *Victoria & Albert Museum.*

66
Stoneware vase, carved and incised and coloured green and brown, inscribed *Martin Bros., London & Southall* and dated *10–1899*. Ht. $8\frac{1}{2}$ in. *Victoria & Albert Museum.*

Page 123

67. Walter, Wallace and Edwin Martin at work in their studio at Southall in 1910. Photograph printed on a wooden panel in *Kingston-upon-Thames Museum and Art Gallery.* (*Victoria & Albert Museum copy*).

illustrative; in such cases one can appreciate the modeller's style and skill without distraction (Plate 60).

Most of the Martin production, however, consisted of vases and similar decorative wares. During forty years their style of making and decorating pottery naturally changed in many respects and, seen in perspective, it seems that their work falls into three main phases.

The pottery made during the first few years at Southall was very similar in style to the work at Pomona House. The shapes tended to be angular and a little awkward. Much of the decoration was carved in relief, as well as incised, and it was bordered with deeply cut or stamped patterns. The predominant colour often used for emphasising the relief patterns against a grey stoneware ground was cobalt blue. This was the style of work which to their later contemporaries seemed crudely old-fashioned; yet, seen in the context of the other stonewares of the time, it has a strength and significance of its own. To the collector the wares of this early phase have the added significance of being rare and of considerable documentary interest.

The second phase of the brothers' pottery began in the early 'eighties and lasted until the mid-'nineties. The angular shapes and those with complicated profiles were mostly replaced by simple rounded, and often globular, shapes. Cut or impressed border patterns were used sparingly and carving in relief became unusual. The patterns were mainly incised and were given emphasis by a contrast of colour. The blue colouring, which had been much used in the 'seventies, was now out of favour and was supplanted by a deep brown; the method of using the colour changed with the nature of the patterns, so that now the ground of the pattern might be given a dark-brown colouring against which the pattern itself would be left in the natural light-fawn colour of the glazed body. This was the period during which W. E. Willey was working at Southall, and it can be presumed that he was largely concerned with the flat incised patterns which were so frequent in this phase.

Probably the commonest style of incised decoration at this time consisted of Renaissance patterns of formally arranged foliage, and these sometimes included highly stylised motifs of dragons. A Martin vase of 1886 with incised Renaissance motifs is illustrated on Plate 61. The smoothly rounded shapes were suitable for this style of decoration; sometimes it was used on the Renaissance ewer shape, which with its narrow neck and up-surging lip must have been exceedingly difficult to fire. Another style, which was much used at this time, consisted of loose arrangements of naturalistically drawn flowers and foliage. These patterns were arranged asymmetrically in a style which was derived from the current enthusiasm for Japanese art. On Martin pottery, however, they do not belong so exactly to the middle phase as do the Renaissance patterns. Examples had appeared occasionally in the 'seventies, and flat loose patterns of this sort had certainly been used by Cazin on some of the pottery that he had made at Fulham. An example of Martin pottery decorated in this attractive style is shown on Plate 62. In this example it appears on a bulbous pot with a tight neck and without a footring, typical of this phase. When the surface of a pot was cut in relief, as in the case of the vase illustrated in Plate 64, the patterns of foliage and flowers tended for this reason to be relatively small in scale and evenly disposed over the surface of the pot. Occasionally, and particularly in the later 'eighties, small birds appear on the pots drawn with an incised line in a manner which is curiously different from that of Wallace's humanised bird models (Plate 63).

In some respects the small bird designs, and especially those drawn on a light ground and using naturalistic colours, may be said to foreshadow the major change of outlook in the Martin designs which occurred about the middle of the 'nineties and which ushered in the last main phase of the brothers' work. They now had available a remarkably wide range of colours such as has scarcely been attempted on saltglazed stoneware before or since. In the later 'nineties the Martin pots were often decorated with dragons, which were drawn freely in a somewhat Far Eastern manner and were widely spaced on attractively coloured and figured grounds. The example illustrated in Plate 65 is on a vase with the high-shouldered shape which had suddenly become by far the commonest shape in the brothers' production. Marine life was another source of inspiration. Fish had been used in the 'eighties, but from the later 'nineties they became one of the commonest subjects. Usually they had comic human expressions on their faces and were depicted on a light green or blue ground to suggest water.

Probably the most attractive pots in this last phase are those in which the interest is concentrated on elaborate surface textures. Sometimes the pottery was given a texture which was abstract in effect; but the general aim of pottery of this sort was to imitate or suggest a vegetable surface, and usually this treatment was carried out on pots with vertically ribbed shapes such as were obviously inspired by vegetable forms. Such work was often coloured in shades of green—a colour which had not been much used before—and the surface of a pot might be elaborately carved and painted with the surface details of an imagined plant. These vegetable forms and surfaces date from the later 'nineties, and they were mainly the work of Walter and Edwin, Walter doing most of the throwing and shaping and Edwin most of the decorating. Very likely the appearance of this style of work, and the interest in surface textures generally, were due to the influence of one particular customer for their pottery, a lawyer named Sydney K. Greenslade, who was concerned to persuade the brothers against using elaborate decoration and who took them with him to the Paris Exhibition of 1900. This was the great exhibition of the Art Nouveau style of decoration, and on every side the brothers must have seen organic and especially vegetable forms in almost every medium from furniture to glass. Their own work was, however, already developing in this direction before their visit to Paris. Plate 66 shows an example of a vegetable form which is dated 1899 and it is interesting to notice that this particular piece was originally in S. K. Greenslade's own collection.

This was the period when Wallace was making the well-known "face jugs", which are certainly skilful and were obviously popular in their day. He was also still making his birds and, in a photograph taken at Southall in 1910, he is shown working with a face jug and birds, while Walter is throwing a vase and Edwin is decorating one (Plate 67). But this was near the end of the pottery. Charles had died in 1910. Walter died in 1912, and the remaining brothers found that they missed not only his skill in throwing large vessels but also his chemical knowledge. Edwin continued to make pottery, now usually small in size but often of great beauty. The last firing was in December 1914, only a few months before Edwin's death. Wallace, the eldest, survived until 1923.

Martin ware can nearly always be identified and dated without difficulty. Usually it has the full information as to its origin and date inscribed on it in cursive handwriting and, except for the first few years, the handwriting was usually that of Edwin. The many variations in the form of the signature and the other particulars are listed in Appendix VII; but the basic changes in the form of the signature were simple and followed logically from the development of the partnership. The first pots, fired at the Fulham Pottery in 1873 and 1874, were inscribed "R. W. Martin, Fulham"; those fired at Shepherd's Bush "R. W. Martin, London"; and the first ones at Southall, "R. W. Martin, Southall". After the opening of the shop in London in 1879 the inscription became "R. W. Martin, London & Southall"; then from about 1883 "R. W. Martin & Bros. (or Martin Bros.), London & Southall". This was virtually the final form of the signature, and the great majority of the Martin pots are signed in this way. Only the very last pots fired in 1914, after the shop had closed, show the last significant change in the omission of the word "London".

CHAPTER 8

WILLIAM DE MORGAN

OF ALL the late Victorian potters William De Morgan was the closest to the Arts and Crafts movement and to its equivalent in the fine arts, the pre-Raphaelite school of painting. For De Morgan was an intimate friend of William Morris and of Edward Burne-Jones; and De Morgan's wife, Evelyn, was a painter of some significance in the pre-Raphaelite manner. For many years Morris and his family were frequent visitors to De Morgan's studio and, to those who know Morris's textile designs, the similarity between them and De Morgan's ceramic decoration is obvious. In some respects De Morgan's preoccupation with painting as a method of decoration has placed his work aside from the main development of artist-made pottery, but few of the decorative artists of the period have produced work which is so intrinsically attractive to collectors and connoisseurs.

De Morgan was born in 1839, the son of Augustus De Morgan who was for many years professor of mathematics at University College in London. In 1859 William De Morgan entered the Royal Academy Schools and, in the early 'sixties, he made the acquaintance of William Morris and of other young artists such as Edward Burne-Jones and Dante Gabriel Rossetti. From about 1864 he was concerned with making designs for stained glass; some years later, being dissatisfied with the colours obtained elsewhere, he set up a small kiln in his parents' home at 40, Fitzroy Square. This led to experiments in pottery glazes and decoration; it also led eventually to the roof of the house being set alight. His father had died in 1871 and, in the following year, he moved with his mother and sister Mary to 30, Cheyne Row (then known as 8, Great Cheyne Row) near the river in Chelsea.

Here he began his serious pottery work as the principal of what was in effect a small firm of tile and pottery decorators. He rented number 36, Cheyne Row, known as "Orange House", as a showroom and workshop, and had a number of girls working as tile decorators in another nearby house.

In 1881 William Morris set up his workshops at Merton Abbey near Wimbledon and, in 1882, he was followed by William De Morgan, who bought some land near by and built workshops and kilns. This venture was not, however, so successful for De Morgan as he had expected. He continued to live in Chelsea and kept his showroom in Orange House until 1886, when it was moved to Great Marlborough Street. He was often concerned with his health and was conscious of the strain of travelling daily between Chelsea and Merton. Accordingly, in 1888, he took the opportunity of going into partnership with the architect Halsey Ricardo and of setting up a pottery, known as the Sands End Pottery, in Fulham.

From about 1892 he began, on medical advice, to spend the winters in Florence, and these absences were inevitably harmful to the firm which had been organised so closely under his personal control. He managed, however, to continue during the winters his work on tile decoration, by employing Italians to paint his designs on to papers which were subsequently fired on the tiles in Fulham. At the end of 1898 the partnership with Halsey Ricardo came to an end, since Ricardo, with an active architect's practice, was finding it increasingly difficult to supervise the affairs of the pottery; and about this time the Great Marlborough Street showroom was given up. In 1897 Reginald Blunt had been asked by De Morgan to help in the management, a task which he carried during the three following winters. The pottery was now clearly failing and one can sense the frustration of all who were connected with it from the account in Reginald Blunt's book *The Wonderful Village* (1918). In these last years the firm was known as De Morgan, Iles and Passenger. Frank Iles was De Morgan's kiln-firer; Fred Passenger, with his brother Charles (who may also have been technically a partner), had been painters in his employment since the 'seventies. In 1905 De Morgan retired from active pottery work, and in 1907 the firm came to an end. Frank Iles and the two Passengers continued, however, to decorate pottery in the style to which they were accustomed. It is said that they were working in the Brompton Road until 1911; and later still, from 1921 to 1933, Fred Passenger was painting pottery and tiles at Bushey Heath for a Mrs. Henry Perrin (See Appendix VIII).

To De Morgan it seemed in the early years of the century that his life's work had failed. But the bitterness engendered by the closing of his pottery was miraculously relieved in the last decade of his life by his sudden and quite unexpected success as a novelist. His only previous experience of writing, apart from letters, had been a "Report on the Feasibility of a Manufacture of Glazed Pottery in Egypt" which he produced in 1894 as a result of a visit to Egypt at the Egyptian Government's expense. In 1906 his novel *Joseph Vance*, written almost by accident, proved a great success; this was followed by six more before his death in 1917; two more were finished by his wife and published after his death. For a time he was far better known as a novelist than as a potter. An article written about him by T. P. O'Connor in *T. P.'s Magazine* for December 1911, contains scarcely any mention of his pottery; yet, after another generation, it is his pottery that again seems his significant work.

All contemporary accounts of De Morgan stress the width of his interests and his empirical approach to problems, not only of art but also of engineering and chemistry. In his old age during the First Word War he was concerned with finishes for the wings of aeroplanes and nets for trapping submarines. It is said that at one time he was designing gears for bicycles. His factory at Fulham was filled with his mechanical contrivances. "His power of invention," wrote Halsey Ricardo, "was boundless: almost every article and tool in the place was the outcome of his observation and invention" (quoted in the *Dictionary of National Biography*).

Above all, his originality of mind determined very largely the nature of his work as a potter, for his methods of decorating his tiles and his pots were based on the minimum of borrowed experience. Virtually all his output can be divided into the two categories of ware painted with lustre colours and with the so-called "Persian" colours. Both the decorative processes involved were worked out by prolonged experiments in the early years of his career, and both were original in the sense that the resulting effects were not easily emulated by orthodox potters.

The use of lustre colours implies that the pattern was painted with material which shows a metallic sheen or reflection when held in certain positions to the light. A strong ruby red, derived from copper, would give a metallic ruby reflection; a yellowish grey, derived from silver, might give a bluish silver reflection. The effect was got by painting on the surface of a glaze with a compound which contained a metallic oxide; during firing this was "reduced" by the introduction of burning material into the kiln, so that part of the oxide was changed into the metal itself. The process has been used intermittently since the first lustre-decorated pottery was made in the Near East during the early Middle Ages. In the early nineteenth century it was much used for the decoration of homely cream-coloured wares, and later, on the continent, it was used in the imitation of Hispano-Moresque ware and the Italian Maiolica of the Renaissance. William De Morgan himself did not claim any orginality in the matter, but his contemporaries were inclined to regard his method of lustre painting as a rediscovery and undoubtedly it was the result of a great deal of personal experimentation.

Most of De Morgan's lustre-painted tiles seem to have been intended as individual decorative items rather than as parts of tile groups or panels. They are usually commercial white tiles, such as were used by De Morgan at Chelsea (see page 133), painted with animals or strange beasts. Most of the lustre-painted pots are also decorated on a plain white glazed ground; and many of the earlier examples were, before decoration, the standard products of Staffordshire potteries. Some of the finest of De Morgan's lustre painting was carried out on large flat dishes such as were exported to the East as rice dishes. Lustre painting remained until the end De Morgan's favourite means of decorating pottery vessels, although on tiles it was used less frequently. In the later years the lustre painting was often carried out on blue ground, and this style was probably much used in the last phase of all—after the retirement of Halsey Ricardo. It was a pot of this sort, elegantly shaped and decorated with a vine pattern, that De Morgan elected to hold in his hands when he sat for his portrait to be painted by his wife in 1909, and this pot is now in the Victoria and Albert Museum (Plates 68 and 69).

His other main style of decoration, the painting in "Persian" colours, was based originally on a colour scheme seen on Near-Eastern pottery. The colours were remarkable for their vivid and yet harmonising qualities, blues, greens and turqouises being particularly prominent. A fine two-handled pot, decorated in these colours, was bought by the South Kensington Museum in 1887 and was presumably made at Merton Abbey (Plate 70). Many large dishes were also decorated in the Persian colours; but this decoration was mainly used for the tiles, and panels of tiles, which always formed by far the greatest part of his production.

In the later 'seventies, while he was working in Chelsea, he was commissioned to make tiles for Lord Leighton's house in Kensington, which is now a public museum. The so-called Arab Hall of the house was decorated with antique Near-Eastern tiles. De Morgan was asked to fill the gaps in the various series of tiles, which he did with such skill that one can barely distinguish his work. A little later, while he was still at Chelsea, he was invited to provide tilework for the Tsar's yacht *Livadia*, and in the 'nineties he produced tile panels for no less than six P. & O. liners. Also in the 'nineties Halsey Ricardo used the De Morgan tiles to great effect in the remarkable house which he built for E. R. Debenham (later Sir Ernest Debenham, Bt.) and which also survives in Kensington.

Most of the tiles decorated in Chelsea were bought in the biscuit state from specialist factories, so that De Morgan's part in them was confined to their decoration. The commercial tiles were made of compressed powder in order to ensure homogeneity of material and to reduce the possibility that they might warp during firing. De Morgan had the idea that tiles made in this way were less likely to last than those made by hand from wet clay. Apparently some of the Chelsea tiles were made throughout by De Morgan from clay supplied by the Plumbago Crucible Company of Battersea. In the built-up residential area of Chelsea the amount of firing had necessarily to be limited; but after the move to Merton Abbey all the tiles could be made by hand, and this no doubt was one of the reasons for the move. The two sorts of tiles can easily be distinguished in practice by the fact that the commercial tiles have the usual arrangement of ridges or other regular impressions on the under side, whereas the hand-made ones are usually impressed with one of the De Morgan marks but are otherwise plain.

The method of painting tiles in the Persian colours was quite different from that of painting in the lustre colours. The lustre colours were painted over a glaze which had already been fired, but the Persian colours were fused in one operation between a white ground below and a clear glaze above. The method of carrying out the painting with the Persian colours was peculiar to De Morgan's work and was characteristic of his ingenuity. The original pattern was painted on paper, using the same brushes as would be used in the finished work. An outline drawing was fixed against a sheet of glass, and from this the factory painter could trace the pattern on to a sheet of paper, filling in the details by copying from the original. The tile, which had already received its first biscuit firing, was covered with a ground of white porcelain slip; the painted paper was stuck on to the ground and covered with a dusting of the raw glaze The tile was then given a firing, during which the paper itself disappeared, but the pattern on it was fused into the white ground and covered with the clear glaze. The main advantage of this method was that the character of hand-painted tiles was preserved, whilst the patterns were repeated with some exactness even after the elapse of many years. The use of papers instead of painting directly on to the tiles was also an advantage when large scenic panels of tiles were being prepared, since by cutting up the painting on paper the exact register of the parts of the panel could easily be maintained. But perhaps the greatest advantage which De Morgan personally derived from this method was that, during the later years of his potting career, he was enabled to supervise the painting of the decoration in Florence for tiles which were to be fired in Fulham. Without this means of sending the tile decoration by post during the winter months his career as a potter would have ended much sooner than it did.

Although De Morgan's production was that of a small factory rather than that of a studio potter, he always regarded himself as the sole arbiter of the design of his ware. Only occasionally did he use designs which came directly from others. Dr. Reginald Thompson, who later married his sister Annie, is said to have contributed some of the early animal designs, and the relief tile patterns used in the later years were the work of Halsey Ricardo. Edward Burne-Jones seems to be represented in the design of a dish in the Victoria and Albert Museum, but this would no doubt be a personal creation. William Morris was an important source of ideas, but not of actual designs. De Morgan wrote on one occasion: "Morris never made but three designs for my execution, the 'Trellis and Tulip', the 'Poppy' and another—I forget the name. I never could work except by myself and in my own manner" (quoted by A. M. W. Stirling, *William De Morgan and his Wife*). His bonds with William Morris were probably closer than he realised, but there were, nevertheless, many features of his work which were not shared with Morris. In particular his treatment of animal motifs was a distinguishing feature of De

Morgan's work (Plate 71). His imaginary animals tended to be fabulous and yet quaintly humanised, like the curious ceramic sculptures of Wallace Martin (see page 116). Ships, also imaginary and fabulous, were a recurring motif, perhaps suggested by the nearby shipping on the Thames, as well as by the long sea voyages to Italy in the latter part of his life (Plates 70 and 72).

A writer in the *Portfolio* magazine in 1876 seems already to be describing De Morgan's mature style of decoration: "a bold border of conventional leafage, mingled with curious monsters, quaint of wing and intricate with foliated tails incalculably coiled, encloses a central medallion containing a bird, a serpent, a stag, or a ship." William Morris's daughter, May Morris, who knew De Morgan well, sought in later years to distinguish three phases in the development of his style: an early period of simple and occasionally naïve work; a bold middle period with strong masses enriched with smaller ornament; and a later period of elaborate and intricate work full of curious invention (*Burlington*, XXXI, 1917). But in practice such distinctions can scarcely be used as a sure means of dating his designs. It may be noticed, too, that some of his designs, of tiles especially, were used over a very long period. On one occasion, in a letter quoted by A. M. W. Stirling, he referred despondently to "the incessant reproduction of patterns drawn by me a quarter of a century since".

Like all the decorative artists associated with the Morris movement, De Morgan conceived his painted designs as flat patterns; rarely did he allow any three-dimensional element of shadowing or perspective to intrude. Animals and ships were usually thought of as parts of a whole pattern, and not as objects of decoration in themselves; indeed, as May Morris indicated, he seems often to have deliberately emphasised a background pattern at the expense of the main theme (*Burlington*, XXXI, 1917). An example of this peculiarity of design, and one of the most impressive of all his works, is to be found in the well-known "antelope" dish in the Victoria and Albert Museum. Here the exaggeration of the foliage knits the animal figure admirably into a unified pattern (Plate 73).

A list of the impressed marks which appear on De Morgan pottery and tiles is given in Appendix VIII. Such marks could, of course, only be impressed in the wet clay, and they appear therefore only on pieces which were made as well as decorated in De Morgan's factory.

This excludes the earlier decorated tiles, which were bought as commercially produced blanks. It excludes, also, the white glazed pottery which was bought as blanks for lustre-painted decoration. It should be noticed, however, that many of the lustre-painted pieces made in De Morgan's own body-material are also lacking in impressed marks. In the Fulham period painted marks were used, in addition to the impressed marks, and alongside them can often be found the initials of the individual painters who interpreted De Morgan's designs, notably Fred and Charles Passenger, Joe Juster and J. Hersey.

CHAPTER 9

PAINTED POTTERY

AN IMMENSE number of Victorian wares were decorated by painting in one form or another. Painted decoration was often added as an additional embellishment to printed or relief-modelled wares; throughout the period it was widely used on relatively cheap table-wares; and latterly painted pottery was one of the important media of artist potteries, notably that of William De Morgan (see Chapter 8). In this chapter the discussion of painted wares will be largely confined to those which are primarily of interest for their painting and which were produced in the industrial factories.

Under factory conditions the art of painting on pottery, or earthenware, may be very closely connected with the art of painting on porcelain. In the Staffordshire "Potteries" individual artists moved freely between the different factories, and both pottery and porcelain might well be made in the same factory. Porcelain, as the finer and more expensive ceramic material, naturally tended to be used more readily than pottery for this relatively expensive means of decoration; a full account of the many Victorian artists concerned with porcelain decoration is to be found in Geoffrey A. Godden's companion volume on *Victorian Porcelain.* But the distinction between painting on pottery and porcelain was well understood in Staffordshire and elsewhere. The fine and precise style induced by porcelain was appropriate on pottery only when it was intended to imitate porcelain. Used in its own right painting on pottery naturally tended to be broader and looser in style. It demanded the qualities of an easel painting rather than of a miniature. If only for this reason, painting on pottery tended to be larger in scale and implied greater freedom for the artist, so that the peculiarities of his style were more immediately obvious than they would be if he were following the conventions of painting on porcelain. It implied, also, the very real danger that the artist would regard his pot or dish merely as a canvas on which to paint, without regard to its form. Striving for the largest possible area he might be tempted to overlook the ceramic need for a limit to decoration and the dramatic effect of empty spaces.

The tradition of painting on cream-coloured wares was continued and developed by Wedgwoods in some notable early Victorian work. Wares of this factory were often painted with large-scale flowers and foliage, spreading widely and boldly in a manner reminiscent of some of the Wedgwood printed wares of the same period (see page 35). Less appropriate to the medium, but nevertheless attractively composed, was the painting, usually of tightly bunched floral subjects, which was carried out by William Fifield on Bristol cream wares over a long period around the beginning of Victoria's reign. A late example of his work is illustrated in the jug on Plate 74 which is signed by his initials and dated 1853. On one of the new stoneware bodies one firm in particular was seen to perpetuate the gaudy "Japan" patterning of the 'twenties: "Mason's Ironstone China" was originally made by George and Charles Mason at Lane Delph in Staffordshire, and the association of the style and the name became so close that both have survived together to the present day (Plate 75).

In the middle years of the century interest was developing in historical pottery styles and in particular in the pottery of the Italian and French Renaissance. By a curious twist in commercial practice the name "majolica", which in a historical context implies primarily painted pottery, came to be attached to a style of pottery in which interest is focused on coloured glazes (see Chapter 5). The appearance of the modern majolica at Mintons did, however, also lead to a new interest in pottery painting as distinct from painting on porcelain (see page 94 and Plates 40, 41 and 42). The talented figure and floral painter, Thomas Kirkby, who is said to have painted the porcelain dessert set given by Queen Victoria to the Emperor of Austria from the 1851 Exhibition, was painting on opaque-glazed majolica in the later 'fifties. An example in the Victoria and Albert Museum is illustrated here, in which he follows the precedent of much of the Italian Rennaissance majolica by using almost the whole of the ceramic surface as his "canvas" (Plate 77). It must be confessed that in this instance his broader drawing on pottery seems a good deal less apt than his tiny painting on porcelain.

The most successful and experienced of the pottery painters employed in this country was the Frenchman Emile Lessore, and it was appropriate that most of his employment was with the firm of

FIG. 20. Wedgwood pottery painted by Emile Lessore (*Art Journal* catalogue of the 1862 Exhibition).

Wedgwoods, which specialised in the production of pottery as opposed to porcelain. He was apparently a pupil of Ingres and an established easel painter in Paris before he was employed for ceramic painting at the great French factory of Sèvres. In 1858 he came to England and, after a few months at Mintons, he settled at Wedgwoods. He returned to France in 1863, but continued to paint Wedgwood pottery in France until his death in 1876. Two early examples of his work for Wedgwoods are shown in Plates 76 and 78. His loose, broad manner of drawing is clearly a direct translation into ceramic terms of an attractive easel-painter's style. His work can scarcely be regarded as other than ceramic "pictures" and yet, within that limitation, it is entirely satisfying; his figure compositions are appropriate in scale and his colouring controlled and subdued to the key of an earthenware medium. Of the two specimens illustrated, one is an academic figure composition (Plate 76); the other is in his more usual vein of sketched figure studies in landscape (Plate 78). There is rarely any doubt about the authorship of his work, since his signature appears freely. His pottery painting was an immediate success in this country, and his work was the highlight of the Wedgwood displays at the Exhibitions of London in 1862 (Fig. 20), of Paris in 1867 and of Vienna in 1873.

Meanwhile at Mintons in the later 'sixties a painter named

Edouard Rischgitz was decorating pottery in a manner which clearly has affinities with that of Lessore. An example, with his signature prominently displayed, is illustrated on Plate 79. A little later, in 1872, Mintons engaged another continental painter, William Mussill, who was to remain with the firm for a considerable period. His work was mainly on pottery, and consists of such motifs as flowers, birds and fish (Plate 80).

In this period, Mintons were also seeking the help of British easel painters, who tended naturally to be interested in painting on pottery rather than on porcelain. William Stephen Coleman, an established artist specialising in figure compositions, was apparently employed for a short time by Copelands and was then engaged in 1869 by Mintons. His work was in a refreshingly original style. "This gentleman", wrote an *Art Journal* commentator, "is the first English artist of reputation who has cared to devote attention to the production of original works on pottery by his own pencil. He has, however, successfully solved the problem, how to apply ready and intelligent Art-power of a high-class to the exigencies of decorative pottery in its best and most genuine, because most effective and durable, form." These remarks were made in the context of a review published in 1872 of an "Art-Pottery Studio" which had been set up by Mintons in the previous year. This venture, although short-lived, was to have important effects on the public's taste for pottery painting. The Studio was set up in Kensington, London, in 1871 under Coleman's direction. It included a small group of professional male painters from Mintons' factory in Stoke-on-Trent, but it was sited in Kensington mainly to attract students of both sexes from the London schools of art. On premises between the Royal Albert Hall and the Horticultural Gardens of those days, it was also ideally placed for those who needed the inspiration of nature in the Gardens or of historical art in the nearby South Kensington Museum. The biscuit pottery was brought to the Studio from Mintons' in Stoke; it was given its decoration and subsequent firings at the Studio, using a kiln which was intended to consume its own smoke. Under the direction of Coleman, and no doubt with the technical co-operation of the painters from Stoke, the wares were painted, often with an elaborate combination of underglaze and overglaze techniques. An example of Coleman's own colourful and open style is shown in the plaque illustrated on Plate 81, which was presumably painted at the

68. Portrait of William De Morgan, painted in 1909 by his wife Evelyn.
Mrs. A. M. W. Stirling (Victoria & Albert Museum photograph).

69
Covered vase painted in lustre colours on a blue ground, by William De Morgan. On the base is impressed mark (h) (Appendix VIII). Ht. 12 in. *Victoria & Albert Museum.*

70
Vase painted in 'Persian' colours, by William De Morgan. Bought in 1887 by the South Kensington museum, the vase (unmarked) was presumably made at Merton Abbey. Ht. 12¾ in. *Victoria & Albert Museum.*

Page 142

71. Vase painted in lustre colours, by William De Morgan. On the base is the painted inscription *D M FULHAM 2209 J H* (for the decorator J. Hersey) *10*. Ht. $9\frac{3}{4}$ in. *Victoria & Albert Museum.*

Page 143

72. Vase painted in lustre colours, by William De Morgan. On the base is the painted inscription *W DE MORGAN FULHAM F P* (for the decorator Fred Passenger). The vase was bought by the South Kensington Museum in 1905 and had been made in the early twentieth century. Ht. 23 in. *Victoria & Albert Museum*

Page 144

73
William De Morgan's 'antelope' dish; unmarked commercial earthenware, painted in ruby and silver lustre, probably about 1880–85. Diam. $14\frac{3}{8}$ in.
Victoria & Albert Museum.

74
ver-painted jug
e by the Bristol
of Pountney and
rated by William
ld. The initials
' and the date
are painted
ath the lip.
$4\frac{5}{8}$ in.
ria & Albert
um.

75. Jug of Mason's 'ironstone china', painted with 'Japan' patterning. Ht. $5\frac{1}{8}$ in.
Victoria & Albert Museum.

76

Dish (originally a tazza) painted with a scene of women bathing in a woodland stream by Emile Lessore (signed). The dish bears the impressed mark WEDGWOOD and the factory date-mark for 1861. Diam. 15 in. *Victoria & Albert Museum.*

77

Majolica tazza made by Mintons and painted in brown by Thomas Kirkby. The piece is signed *Kirkby pinx.* and *Minton & Co.*, and on the reverse is a painted inscription *Apotheosis of the Amours of Jupiter from Julia Romano.* It was bought for the South Kensington Museum from the London Exhibition of 1862 Diam. 13½ in. *Victoria & Albert Museum.*

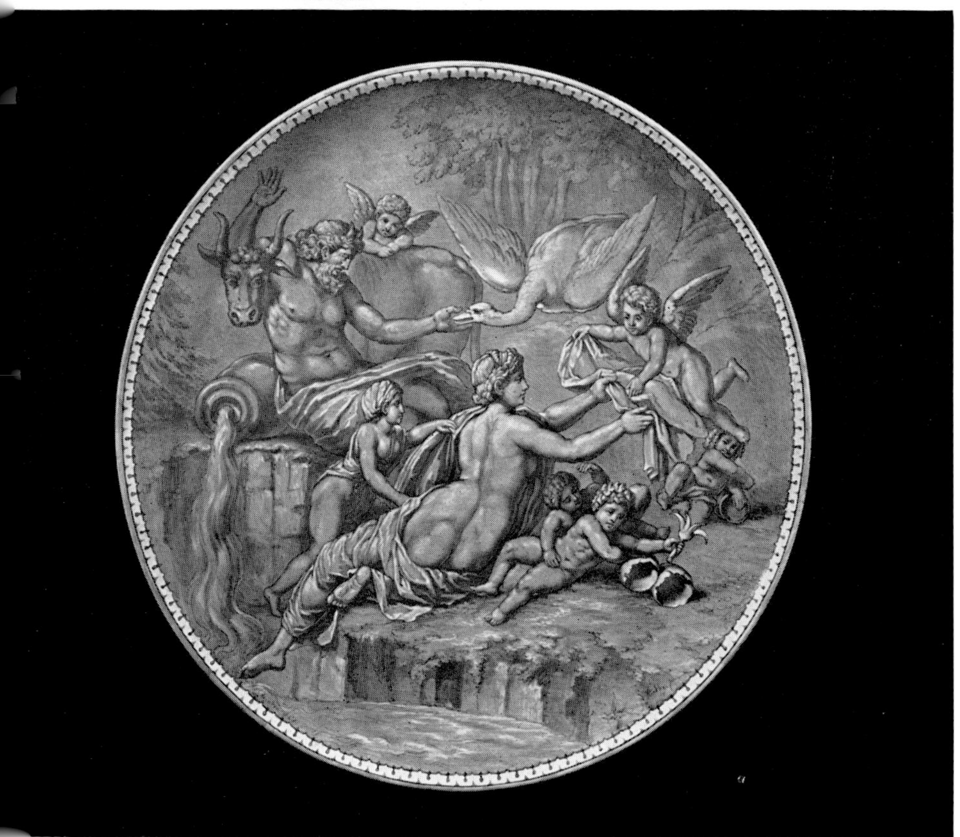

78

Dish painted with figures in a landscape by Emile Lessore (signed). The dish bears the impressed mark WEDGWOOD and the factory date-mark for 1862. Length $11\frac{1}{2}$ in. *Victoria & Albert Museum.*

79

Tazza painted with the subject of the wolf acting as shepherd, by Edouard Rischgitz (signed). On the base are impressed *MINTON* and the factory date-mark for 1863, with the painted inscription *MINTON* and *Le 12 Juillet 1864.* Diam. $10\frac{1}{2}$ in. *Victoria & Albert Museum.*

Studio. He probably exerted a strong influence on the other artists, although they seem to have been free to develop their own designs. Among those who received this training and experience were the Swiss Edmund G. Reuter, who was later to be employed for twenty years as a painter at Mintons' factory, and Hannah B. Barlow, who was very shortly to begin drawing her animals in sgraffito on Doultons' stoneware (see page 99).

The studio was expected to have a great influence on contemporary ceramics. The *Art Journal* commentator of 1872 remarked that "from such a centre we may hope to see the springing up of a really national school of painters in pottery, untrammelled by the mere conventionalities and trade traditions of the past". Unfortunately in 1873 Coleman withdrew from it; in 1875 it was burnt down, and was never rebuilt. But during its short period it attracted much public attention, and its example was obviously an important factor in a remarkable craze for amateur ceramic painting which developed in the 'seventies and 'eighties. The products of the Studio are usually to be recognised by a circular printed mark with the inscription "Mintons' Art-Pottery Studio Kensington Gore" in addition to the Minton marks impressed at the factory.

The subsequent amateur work often bears, also, the Minton impressed marks, since Mintons were the most frequent purveyors of biscuit-fired blanks; and naturally such work bears the signature or initials of the painter. Occasionally a piece may be found which still retains a printed label indicating that it has figured in one of the many exhibitions of amateur work such as those organised by the London firm of Howell & James (Plate 82). Firms such as this organised the supply of pottery blanks, the supply of materials, instructions for using them, the firing of the painted decoration and subsequent exhibitions. The work was by no means all so amateurish as may seem to be implied by the manner of its production, and the best examples are clearly related to the contemporary style of the art schools, as expressed in other flat-pattern designs, rather than to the more specialised styles of Stoke-on-Trent.

A comparison naturally springs to mind between the influence of Mintons' Studio and that of the somewhat similar establishment at Doultons in Lambeth, which produced saltglazed stoneware and later painted "faience" (see Chapter 6). Both were set up in the same period and, although it is difficult to find any direct connection between the two, they were both clearly engendered by the outlook of the art schools. Both expressed in pottery a newly-found respect for the dignity and individuality of the artist-craftsman and were at one with the developing spirit of the Arts and Crafts movement. Ultimately Doultons' studio had the greater effect on the history of British artist pottery, since it dealt more directly with the clay material; but there has also been a continuing, if subsidiary, tradition in the painting of industrial pottery by artists whose outlook is independent of the industrial traditions of the Potteries.

Meanwhile Mintons were seeking to use another established artist's ideas in the production of painted pottery. Henry Stacy Marks was a painter with a bent for depicting humorous Shakespearean subjects, who was to be made a Royal Academician in 1878. Mintons showed some of the work designed by him at the Vienna Exhibition of 1873. A typical example is shown in the vase on Plate 83, which has the factory date-mark for 1877. Such a work shows very clearly the academic easel-painter's approach to the decoration of ceramics with large, suitably composed, scenes.

Easel-painters were not, however, the only artists from beyond the industry who could make a useful contribution. Some of the most successful influences on industrial painted pottery came from the artist-potter William De Morgan and from general designers such as Walter Crane and Lewis Day. All these artists were founder members of the Arts and Crafts Exhibition Society in 1888, and Walter Crane was twice its president. The style and outlook of William De Morgan's own pottery has already been discussed at length (see Chapter 8). His revival of lustre-painted pottery was perhaps the feature of his work which attracted the widest attention, and the use of this technique was taken up most prominently in the decoration of tiles and pottery made under industrial conditions by the firm of Maw & Co. of Jackfield in Shropshire. Maws made a great display of their tilework, which included designs by both Walter Crane and Lewis Day, at the Royal Jubilee Exhibition at Manchester in 1887, and also at the other Exhibitions of the late 'eighties at Adelaide in 1887, Glasgow in 1888 and Melbourne in 1888–9. About the same time Walter Crane was experimenting on Wedgwoods' cream-coloured ware; the vases shown on Plate 84 are dated 1888, and may perhaps have been decorated by his own hand. His most striking pottery designs were perhaps for Maws, in which he excelled in producing figure motifs for painting in ruby lustre on strongly curving shapes (Plate 85). Later, in the first decade of the twentieth century, he was also making designs for the well-known lustre-painted pottery of the Pilkington firm, of Clifton Junction near Manchester; and, like his pottery designs for Wedgwoods and for Maws, these can be readily recognised by his personal monogram of a crane bird.

CHAPTER 10

ART POTTERIES

IN ITS widest sense the phrase "art pottery" might be taken to apply to all decorative wares; but in later Victorian times, when it was most current, the phrase carried with it the implication of pottery which was deliberately creative or artistic. Art pottery in this context was likely to reflect the intellectual "aesthetic" approach of the period and to interpret in a more or less popular sense the ideas of the Arts and Crafts movement. Some of the most effective of the art pottery has already been discussed in the chapters on Doultons' factory in Lambeth, the Martin brothers and William De Morgan. There remain, however, a number of late Victorian art potters and potteries whose work is often attractive and whose ideas made a serious contribution to the ceramic history of the period.

In the north-east of England and in the north Midlands three men produced between them a group of wares of great distinction and originality. They were the potters Henry Tooth and William Ault and the professional designer Christopher Dresser. Henry Tooth began his potting career as effective head of a new pottery at Linthorpe near Middlesbrough, which was set up in the late 'seventies by John Harrison (Plates 86 and 87). Tooth had been a man of many occupations and, during the 'sixties, he had worked in London as a theatrical scene-painter. Clearly he came to pottery with a fresh and original outlook and, in spite of lack of previous training, his approach seems to have been that of a practical potter with an especial interest in colours and glazes. From the first the enterprise at Linthorpe was connected, also, with the name of Christopher Dresser, who was already well known as a freelance professional designer. In the course of his career he was to produce much important work, not only for pottery but for textiles, wallpapers, metal-work, furniture and glass. His designs for small three-dimensional objects, particularly in pottery and silver, were always original and were often somewhat angular in a style reminiscent of some pre-

Columbian American pottery. His fame was sufficient for his impressed signature to appear beside the Linthorpe stamp on the wares which he designed for that pottery. The letters HT in monogram, for Henry Tooth, also appear alternatively or in addition to Dresser's signature, on some of the early Linthorpe ware. Tooth's part was, however, mostly in the development of multicoloured "flowing" glazes. These glaze effects, often used as the sole surface-decoration of ornamental pottery, represented a new line of development which in this country was perhaps first explored at Linthorpe. In view of the many different glaze effects which have been elaborated under Far Eastern influence in the early twentieth century, the Linthorpe glazes may now pass almost unnoticed, but in their own day they achieved an immediate impact on Christopher Dresser's forms. According to Llewellynn Jewitt's near-contemporary account in his *Ceramic Art of Great Britain* (2nd edn. 1883), the pottery was founded in 1879; and already in 1880 the work was being noted in the *Art Journal* and linked with the Japanese style which was then at the height of fashion. Jewitt commented: "These works . . . are characterised by a purity of art-treatment not found elsewhere", although he clearly disliked Christopher Dresser's forms. Henry Tooth must have left Linthorpe in 1882; and it is significant that, again according to Jewitt, Christopher Dresser's designs and his signature were only used during the first three or four years. The Linthorpe factory continued to use the glazes on pottery of more conventional shapes, but their effect was somewhat spoiled by the multiplication of other methods of surface decoration, especially of painting and sgraffito work.

About 1882 Henry Tooth went into partnership with William Ault and, in 1883, the Bretby Art Pottery was established at Woodville in south Derbyshire; but it is said that the two men with strong and independent characters could not work together and, in 1887, William Ault set up his own pottery at Swadlincote, also in the south Derbyshire area and within a few miles of Woodville. Much of the style and emphasis of William Ault's pottery, known as "Ault Faience", was reminiscent of Linthorpe ware; in the years about 1892 to 1896 Christopher Dresser was again concerning himself with pottery in a series of designs which he produced for William Ault. Like the earlier Linthorpe wares, this pottery made to Dresser's designs is easily recognised, since it is stamped on the base with

Dresser's signature. The vase illustrated on Plate 88 is typical of this second phase of an exotic influence on late Victorian pottery.

Another group of late Victorian "art potteries" was to be found in Devon. From this county came the Barum and Aller Vale wares which ultimately achieved the distinction of being described and illustrated in the catalogues of Liberty's of Regent Street, the most influential fashion-makers of the end of the century. Even Watcombe pottery, near Torquay (see page 80) was obliged to add to its chaste terracottas some heavily painted wares and bizarre shapes in the current art-pottery fashion. Barum ware was made in Barnstaple, and was called Barum after the Roman name for that town. It came from a pottery which was established in 1879 by Charles H. Brannam, whose father had made rough kitchenware elsewhere in the town. The development of the pottery was helped by the London dealers Howell & James, with the effect that it received royal patronage in 1885 (J. F. Blacker, *Nineteenth-century English Ceramic Art*). Most of the Barum ware appeared in natural thrown shapes and its decoration was often in sgraffito or painted slips (Plate 89 and see page 157); as such it had certainly more affinity with the traditional country wares than most of the other fashionable art wares of the latter part of the century. Much of the decoration was, however, in line with the normal art-pottery style, depending for its effect on rich colouring and glaze. C. H. Brannam is said to have done all his own throwing, whilst the decoration was carried out by others, among whom J. Dewdney was prominent. The pottery was normally signed by C. H. Brannam with a cursive inscription on the base. The date was often added, as were the initials of the decorator, such as JD in monogram for J. Dewdney.

The Aller Vale wares were made near Newton Abbot. The factory had previously made architectural wares, and a change was made to art pottery in 1881 when it was rebuilt after a fire. The decorating artists came from a local school of art, which was flourishing when the art pottery was initiated. The ware was heavily decorated on fashionably affected shapes. An article on Devonshire potteries, published in the *Art Journal* in 1900, gives a list of the Aller Vale wares—the "motto" ware and "grotesques", wares with the titles "Sandringham" and "Abbots Kerswell", and, the latest of all, the "Crocus" ware, in which tall shapes were decorated in an almost Art Nouveau manner with a pattern of giant crocus flowers.

In the neighbouring county of Somerset Sir Edmund Elton was producing his "Elton Ware", which was characteristic of the late nineteenth-century art potteries although it was produced virtually under studio conditions. The pottery was made at the Elton family home, Clevedon Court, mainly with the help of an assistant, George Masters, who, like Elton himself, had received no professional pottery training. Elton is said to have come to pottery with the mildly revolutionary ideas of the pre-Raphaelites. His first pottery was made in the early 'eighties (a piece at Clevedon Court is dated 1882), and he was still actively potting at the time of his death in 1920. Throughout this long period the variation in style seems relatively slight and, as his work is not usually dated, it is often difficult to assign a piece to a particular decade. Although some examples of openwork decoration are known, his most usual style, especially in the period before the end of the nineteenth century, was characterised by asymmetrical relief patterns of flowers and foliage built up of coloured slips with sgraffito outline. His ground colours were usually mottled shades of blue, blended perhaps with greens (Plate 90). Another style of Elton ware, often encountered, has a heavily crackled metallic finish, but this was probably not used until after 1900. In some degree Elton's work of the later 'eighties and 'nineties can probably be distinguished from his subsequent work by the freedom of form which he shared, even to excess, with the other art potteries of the time. In an article on Elton ware which appeared in the *Art Journal* in 1901 the writer, Charles Quentin, remarks: "He has produced some beautiful forms, but now and then tends a little too much towards the quaint." If one looks at the illustrations to the article, one can see the force of this remark, especially in the profusion of oddly shaped and oddly placed handles on the wares that Elton had been producing at that time.

In the last years of the nineteenth century a pottery, was operating in Birkenhead which professed the highest "artistic" principles. It was founded by Harold Rathbone, a member of a prominent local family and a painter pupil of Ford Madox Brown. It was called the Della Robbia pottery, a name which besides its obvious reference to the Italian Renaissance, implied the use of opaque-glazed ware. The Birkenhead pottery was working only from 1894 to 1906, but it attracted a good deal of attention and royal patronage. The products were of two sorts—architectural "faience" and hollow pottery wares.

The architectural faience consisted mostly of attractive decorative panels modelled with figure subjects in high relief, Some of these were modelled by the well-known sculptor R. Anning-Bell. Others were by Conrad Dressler, Miss E. M. Rope, and Harold Rathbone himself.

Of more interest to collectors, however, are the hollow wares of this Birkenhead pottery. These are remarkable for their colouring, which is usually based on a vivid green, and for their shapes, which are sometimes original to the point of being grotesque. The methods of decoration are nearly always a combination of sgraffito and painting (Plates 91 and 92). Nearly all of the artists employed had been art school students. Great respect was paid to their individuality as artists and, following the example of other art potteries and especially of Doultons, they were expected to sign their work by initials or monogram. Thus a pot will often bear a sgraffito mark to indicate the artist who carried out the sgraffito decoration, together with a painted mark to indicate the artist responsible for the painted colouring; this would be in addition to the sgraffito factory mark of a medieval sailing ship and the letters D and R for Della Robbia. A considerable number of artists were working in the pottery at various times and their individual marks cannot always be identified with any certainty. Among the more common marks are LW, which represents Liza Wilkins, and C, which apparently represents Charles Collis, two artists who were both with the pottery for the greater part of its existence. Other marks often met with are RB for Ruth Bare and CAW for Casandia Ann Walker. One of the artists associated with the project was the sculptor Carlo Manzoni, and it is interesting to notice that in the years about 1896 he was responsible for a small pottery at Hanley, called the Granville pottery, the wares of which are found with painted sgraffito decoration and Manzoni's initials in monogram (Plate 93). It is known that he moved his home from Hanley to Birkenhead in the later 'nineties, and it may be that his experience was a determining factor in the style of the Della Robbia pottery.

CHAPTER 11

COUNTRY POTTERIES

MANY of the potteries discussed in the last chapter were of the "country" in the sense that they were situated away from the "Potteries" of Staffordshire and from other large towns. They were, however, all making at least some wares which were relatively sophisticated in their appeal, and which were intended to achieve a general sale and appreciation. All the potteries considered in this chapter might more properly be regarded as country potteries. Some of their wares were also ambitious and consciously "artistic", but in general they were the potteries whose wares were mainly traditional and directed to a local market.

A glance at the closely printed pages of Llewellynn Jewitt's *Ceramic Art of Great Britain*, first published in 1877, will give some indication of the immense number of small potteries scattered about the country, which were continually changing their names and their wares throughout the nineteenth century. Many of them are scarcely known today except from a few chance specimens which may survive in a local museum or in the homes of the potters' descendants; but mostly these obscure wares are marked or can be easily recognised in the locality, and they offer to the collector an opportunity to form very cheaply a collection which will certainly be of local interest, and which may prove later to have some general historical significance. In this account it will only be possible to mention a few country wares of particular interest which the author has encountered in museum collections.

The traditions of country pottery have mostly survived through the style of earthenware known as slipware. The name implies that the ware is decorated with slip, or liquid clay, and for this purpose the colour of the slip must contrast with that of the body. The slip may be used decoratively in several different ways, of which the two most prominent are those of trailing and of sgraffito. By the trailing method a dark brown pot is patterned, or given an inscription, by trails of white or light-brown slip, and the trails are formed by squeezing the slip through an aperture in the manner by which one applies an inscription to an iced cake. By the sgraffito method the dark brown pot is dipped into the white slip; when the slip is dry, it is cut away to reveal the dark body below and, hence, the pattern is in brown slightly recessed against a white ground. With slipware the decoration is all carried out before any firing has taken place and it is therefore entirely under the glaze, and the glaze has usually a brownish or a greenish cast, so that on the finished pottery the white lines or areas appear either honey-coloured or else a thin green. The green glaze seems to have been mainly a nineteenth-century innovation, but slipware with the honey-coloured glaze had been the staple decorative ware of the country potteries since the seventeenth century. In the latter part of the eighteenth century and in the nineteenth century its popularity was receding, but it has survived into the twentieth century to become a direct source of inspiration to modern artist-potters. In this sequence the slipware of the Victorian period is the least known; yet it has survived in fair quantity and includes many pieces which in a naïve manner are greatly attractive.

Probably the richest area of the country for the collector of slipware is the south-west, and especially the county of Devon. In this area, which is incidentally much favoured by artist-potters today, the traditions of slipware pottery continued strongly into the nineteenth century. The potters were mostly concerned in their everyday work with the production of kitchen wares but they made a wide range of decorative pottery for special occasions and their particular pride in this area was their finely decorated harvest jugs. Excellent examples can be seen in the Burton Art Gallery at Bideford and in the Exeter Museum. Some of those in the Bideford Gallery are signed by slipware potters who worked in Bideford East-the-Water, such as a jug by Earnest [*sic*] Phillips dated 1874 and two examples by Henry Phillips dated 1881. But the best-known family of potters in this region were the Fishleys who worked at Fremington, between Bideford and Barnstaple. Early nineteenth-century pieces known or presumed to have been made by a George Fishley are in the Art Gallery at Bideford and in the Athenaeum at Barnstaple; in the Exeter Museum there is a harvest jug inscribed "Edmund Fishley Maker Jan 6th 1839". Later in the century Edwin Beer Fishley was working at Fremington until his death in 1912 and he has left many fine pots signed with his name. The plate illustrated here (Plate 94) is decorated in sgraffito with a simple cursive motif, in a manner which is unmistakably ancestral to a good deal of the sophisticated slipware of the present time.

Other slipware potteries survived, and indeed thrived, in the north of England. In the Grosvenor Museum in Chester can be seen a collection of Buckley Ware, with sgraffito or applied slip decoration. The examples include a bowl dated 1863 and a puzzle jug of 1873 (Plate 95). This ware was made in a few potteries in Flintshire and sold in Chester. Another such ware was made at Denholme near Bradford in Yorkshire; and examples can be seen in the Bolling Hall Museum at Bradford, bearing the dates 1826, 1856 and 1878 (Plate 96).

Another district in which rural potteries have survived into modern times is in the south-east of England, especially in Sussex. Here the many local potteries were scattered over a wide area, but the most notable were those at Rye. The attractive Sussex pottery with inlaid slip patterns was mainly, if not entirely, pre-Victorian in date; but, if the Victorian wares included little of slip decoration, they have often the surface interest of a pleasantly speckled glaze, which arises from traces of iron in the clay body. Vigorously shaped harvest jugs and "turnip" money-boxes were perhaps the most typical products. From Brede came a series of delightfully modelled hedgehog figures; from the Cadborough pottery near Rye, and later from the Bellevue pottery in the same town, came the well-known "Sussex pigs". The latter were supposedly a combination of jugs with cups, moulded in the form of pigs with detachable heads, and they were deliberately given a speckled effect, apparently by the splashing of manganese (Plate 98). A more ambitious ware from the same pottery was ponderously over-decorated with separately moulded motifs, which were coloured in green against the brown of the body and usually represented sprays of hops.

The pottery which came from Castle Hedingham, in Essex, should be mentioned here, although it can scarcely be considered a normal product of rural craftsmanship. It is often encountered and is quite unmistakable, both because of its strongly individual style and because it is well marked with the initials of the potter and the symbol of a castle. It was made by Edward Bingham, the son of a potter who had come to the Castle Hedingham in the eighteen-thirties.

For a time about the early 'sixties the young Edward Bingham was running a school, but he continued his interest in his father's craft and, in 1864, he is said to have been employing several assistants in his pottery. Later, with his son E. W. Bingham, he began to specialise in making individual ornamental pieces. In this he must have been given a good deal of support by the interest of various members of the Royal Archaeological Society—including Sir Henry Cole and Sir A. W. Franks—when the Society visited Hedingham, to see the castle, in 1876. Some of his pieces were bought from an exhibition in Hertford in 1880 by John Sparkes, who had been much concerned in the initiation of the Doulton art pottery (see page 96) and was by this time the headmaster of the National Art Training School at South Kensington (Henry Clay, *Connoisseur*, XCIV, 1934). This august interest on the part of connoisseurs of artist pottery is perhaps a little surprising, since Bingham's individual pieces were engagingly imaginative and amusing but scarcely ever serious in the art-school sense. The teapot illustrated on Plate 97 is by no means exceptional in the fantasy of its treatment.

Apart from the rural potteries making simple earthenwares, there were many other local potteries which specialised in such wares as Rockingham and cane ware and in saltglazed stoneware; and some of them continue today with those products. The word "Rockingham" defined a ware with a manganese-brown glaze which had been used at the Rockingham works in the early part of the nineteenth century (see page 93). It was much used for teapots and other kitchen wares, and was associated especially with the curious "Cadogan" teapots which were lidless and filled from a hole in the base. The cane ware consisted mainly of such kitchen objects as pressed mixing bowls. A number of potteries making wares of this sort were flourishing in Scotland. The Dunmore pottery, near Stirling, was making Rockingham and other coloured-glaze wares; the Rosslyn pottery at Kirkcaldy made Rockingham and cane wares and at one time was known for its money-boxes in the form of animals and houses; and the pottery at Alloa was apparently making Rockingham wares throughout Victoria's reign. After the fashion for lustre painting had receded in early Victorian times, Rockingham and similar wares were the mainstay of the small potteries of the Sunderland district, such as Ball's, Rickaby's and Bridge End potteries. A similar group of local potteries was to be found on the

Tees, in Stockton and Middlesbrough, and again in South Wales, especially in Swansea. Another group, and perhaps the most interesting, was concentrated in the south Derbyshire villages of Woodville, Church Gresley and Swadlincote. This area was the home of the art pottery of William Ault and Henry Tooth (see page 153), but it was also the source of a distinctive style of teapots which is most attractive to collectors.

The south Derbyshire teapots were decorated in a highly characteristic manner with applied figures of birds and flowers which were painted in various colours. Many of them were very large and these had a knob on the lid in the form of a minature teapot. A typical example is illustrated in Plate 99 and, like many others, this bears an inscription which has been impressed in the clay with disused printer's type. In spite of the impression of antiquity given by the style of lettering and by the garish painting, these teapots clearly belong to the end rather than the beginning of the century. The late Pascoe H. Tunnicliff, son of the one-time owner of the Victoria pottery in Woodville, recalled (in a private letter) that the teapots were being made at his father's pottery "from 1890, or perhaps earlier, until 1910", and that "they were also made by Mason Cash & Co. Church Gresley, and other works in the district in earlier years". Although teapots predominate, other objects were made in the same style, such as a kettle and a jug in Oldham Museum. The latter has an inscription, no doubt made to order, consisting of a personal name followed by "Oldham 1883".

APPENDIX I

REGISTRY MARKS

Objects designed between 1842 and 1883 often bear a lozenge-shaped mark which indicates that they were registered at the Patent Office Design Registry. The mark provides a key whereby the name of the person or firm effecting the registration can be obtained from official records, whilst the date of registration can be deduced from the codes at (*a*) and (*b*) below. It should be noticed that in this period ceramic objects were always listed as Class IV.

After 1883 a new series of registrations began which are indicated on the object by a serial number. Beginning at 1 in 1884 the numbers had reached some 368,000 by the end of the century. At (*c*) below are listed the first registrations issued in each year of objects in all classes. Before the beginning of 1892, however, account should be taken of a slight numerical overlap between the registrations of each December and January.

(*a*) 1842 to 1867

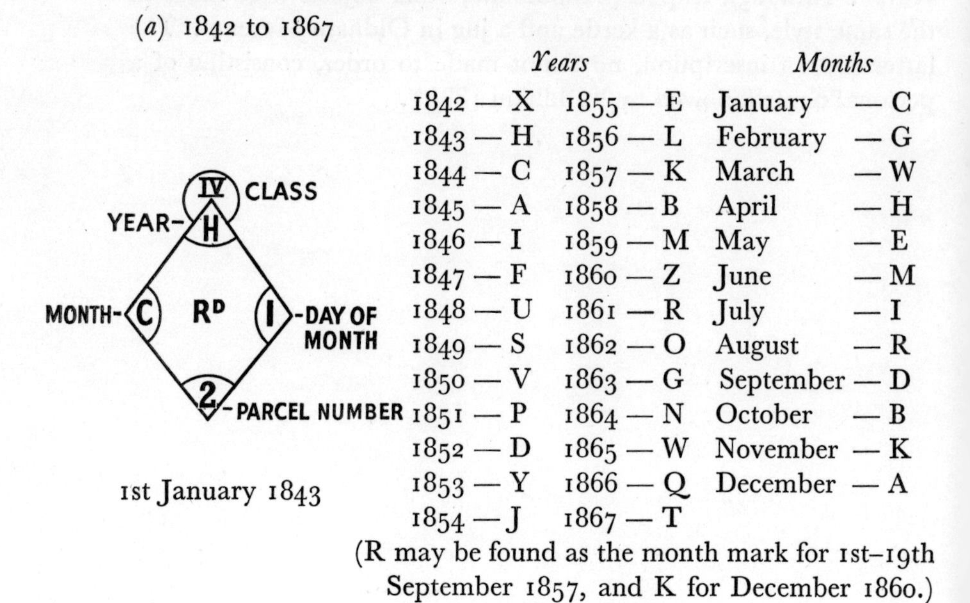

1st January 1843

Years		*Months*	
1842 — X	1855 — E	January	— C
1843 — H	1856 — L	February	— G
1844 — C	1857 — K	March	— W
1845 — A	1858 — B	April	— H
1846 — I	1859 — M	May	— E
1847 — F	1860 — Z	June	— M
1848 — U	1861 — R	July	— I
1849 — S	1862 — O	August	— R
1850 — V	1863 — G	September	— D
1851 — P	1864 — N	October	— B
1852 — D	1865 — W	November	— K
1853 — Y	1866 — Q	December	— A
1854 — J	1867 — T		

(R may be found as the month mark for 1st–19th September 1857, and K for December 1860.)

(*b*) 1868 to 1883

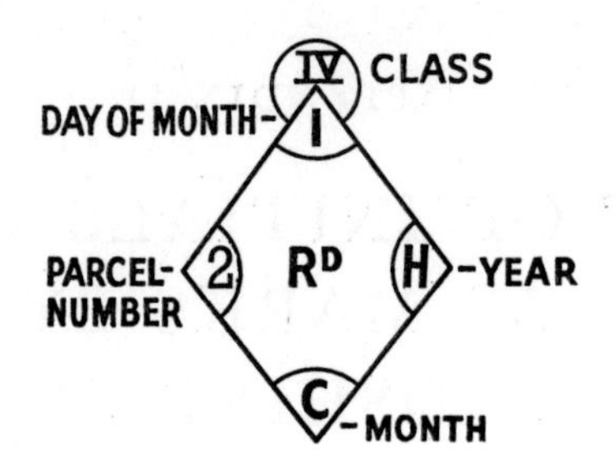

1st January 1869

Years		*Months*	
1868 — X	1876 — V	January	— C
1869 — H	1877 — P	February	— G
1870 — C	1878 — D	March	— W
1871 — A	1879 — Y	April	— H
1872 — I	1880 — J	May	— E
1873 — F	1881 — E	June	— M
1874 — U	1882 — L	July	— I
1875 — S	1883 — K	August	— R
		September	— D
		October	— B
		November	— K
		December	— A

(For 1st–6th March 1878, G was used for the month and W for the year.)

(*c*) 1884 to 1901

1884 — 1	1890 — 141273	1896 — 268392
1885 — 19754	1891 — 163767	1897 — 291241
1886 — 40480	1892 — 185713	1898 — 311658
1887 — 64520	1893 — 205240	1899 — 331707
1888 — 90483	1894 — 224720	1900 — 351202
1889 — 116648	1895 — 246975	1901 — 368154

APPENDIX II

LIST OF INITIALS USED AS MARKS BY STAFFORDSHIRE POTTERS

The following list has been taken from information compiled by the late Alfred Meigh from directories and rate-books, and has been revised by Geoffrey A. Godden the present owner of Meigh's material and its copyright. The list is substantially confined to the nineteenth century; where potters' dates are shown as continuing into the twentieth century, this should not be taken to imply that the initials continued in use or continued in the same form. Dates left open mean that the firms are still in existence.

Initials	Potter
A Bros	G. L. Ashworth Bros. (now at Hanley) (Shelton, 1862–)
A & B	Adams & Bromley (Shelton, 1873–94)
A B & Co	Allman, Broughton & Co. (Burslem, 1861–74)
A B & Co H	A. Bullock & Co. (Hanley, 1880–1915)
A & Co	Edward Asbury (Longton, 1875–1925)
A J M	A. J. Mountford (Burslem, 1898–1902)
B over an anchor	British Anchor Pottery Co. (Longton, 1884–)
B B	Barker Bros (Longton, 1876–82)
B & B	Bates & Bennett (Cobridge, 1868–85)
B & B	Blackhurst & Bourne (Burslem, 1880–92)
B & B	Bridgett & Bates (Longton, 1882–1915)
B B B	Bridgett, Bates & Beech (Longton, 1875–82)
B B W & M	Bates, Brown-Westhead & Moore (Shelton, 1859–61)
B & C	Bridgwood & Clarke (Burslem & Tunstall, 1858–64)

80
Vase painted by William Mussill; made by Mintons with factory date-mark for 1876. Ht. 13 in. *Minton's Museum, Stoke-on-Trent (Pottery Gazette and Glass Trade Review photograph).*

81
[...]que painted by W. S. [...]eman (signed); on the [...]rse is impressed the [...]ton date-mark for 1871 [...] a printed mark inscribed *[...]NTON'S Art-Pottery [...]DIO Kensington Gore.* [...]m. 15 in. *Mr. Geoffrey [...]den.*

82. Plate painted by an amateur painter, Miss F. Wyllie, from Howell & James' Art Pottery Exhibition, 1883. On the reverse are the painted initials of the artist and an exhibition label. Diam. 12½ in. *Mrs. A. Mangan.*

83
Vase, with painted decoration of medieval figures designed by H. Stacy Marks. The vase bears the impressed mark MINTONS and the factory date-mark for 1877. Ht. 14 in. *Victoria & Albert Museum.*

84. Two identical vases with painted decoration by Walter Crane, impressed WEDGWOOD with date-mark for 1888; both are inscribed 'Imagination' and one bears the Crane monogram. Ht. 10 in. *Wedgwood Museum, Barlaston.*

85. Vase painted in ruby lustre, made by Maw & Co., Jackfield, and designed by Walter Crane about 1889. On the base is painted the Crane monogram. Ht. 9 in. *Victoria & Albert Museum.*

86
Vase with incised decoration and figured glaze, designed by Christopher Dresser for the Linthorpe pottery, near Middlesbrough, about 1880. On the base are the marks *LINTHORPE* and *Chr. Dresser* impressed. Ht. 6½ in. *Dorman Memorial Museum, Middlesbrough.*

87
Vase with figured greenish glaze and relief flowers picked out in white and purple, designed by Christopher Dresser for the Linthorpe pottery, near Middlesbrough, about 1880. The vase bears on the base the marks *LINTHORPE* and *Chr. Dresser* impressed, and also HT in monogram (for Henry Tooth). Ht. 18 in. *Dorman Memorial Museum, Middlesbrough.*

88
Vase with figured green glaze, designed by Christopher Dresser for William Ault's pottery, Swadlincote, 1892–96. On the base is the facsimile signature *Chr. Dresser.* Ht. $10\frac{1}{2}$ in *Victoria & Albert Museum*

89
Barum-ware jug with blue slip decoration, made by C. H. Brannam, Barnstaple. On the base is the inscription *C. H. Brannam, Barum, N. Devon,* the date 1884 and *JD* in monogram (for J. Dewdney.) Ht. $5\frac{3}{8}$ in. *Victoria & Albert Museum.*

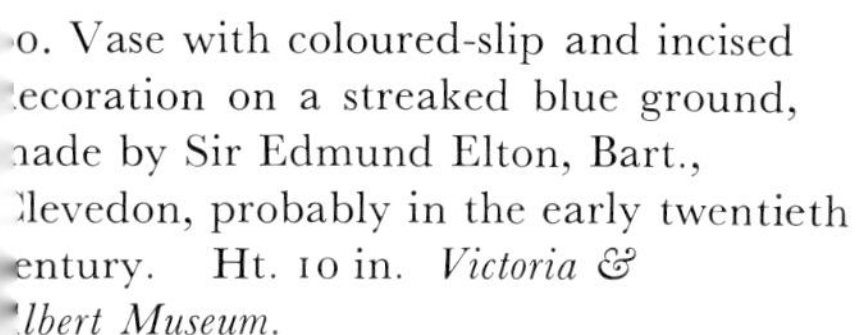

ɪo. Vase with coloured-slip and incised
:ecoration on a streaked blue ground,
ɪade by Sir Edmund Elton, Bart.,
:levedon, probably in the early twentieth
entury. Ht. 10 in. *Victoria &*
:lbert Museum.

91. Vase with painted sgraffito decoration and an inscription recording a presentation in 1899, made by the Della Robbia pottery, Birkenhead. On the base, besides the sgraffito of a ship and *DR* (for Della Robbia), are the decorator's initials *C* sgraffito (for Charles Collis) and *LW* painted (for Liza Wilkins). Ht. 15¼ in. *Williamson Art Gallery and Museum, Birkenhead.* (*Victoria & Albert Museum photograph.*)

92
Jug with painted sgraffito decoration, made by the Della Robbia pottery, Birkenhead. On the base are the sgraffito mark of a ship, the sgraffito initials *CAW* (for the decorator Casandia Ann Walker) and the date 1897. Ht. $10\frac{3}{4}$ in. *Williamson Art Gallery and Museum, Birkenhead* (*Victoria & Albert Museum photograph*).

93
Vase with painted sgraffito decoration, made by the Granville Pottery. On the base are the initials *CM* in monogram (for Carlo Manzoni) and the date 1895. Ht. 9 in. *Victoria & Albert Museum.*

B C Co	Britannia China Co. (Longton, 1895–1906)
B & Co	Birks & Co. (Longton, 1896–9)
B & Co	Boulton & Co. (Longton, 1892–1902)
B E & Co	Bates, Elliot & Co. (Burslem, 1870–5)
B F	Benjamin Floyd (Lane End, 1843)
B G P Co	Brownfield Guild Pottery Co. (Cobridge, 1894–1900)
B G & W	Bates, Gildea & Walker (Burslem, 1878–81)
B & H	Bednall & Heath (Hanley, 1879–1901)
B & H	Blackhurst & Hulme (Longton, 1890–1932)
B & K	Barkers & Kent (Fenton, 1889–1941)
B & L	Burgess & Leigh (Burslem, 1862–)
B & M	Bagshaw & Meir (Burslem, 1802–08)
B M & T	Boulton, Machin & Tennant (Tunstall, 1889–99)
B P Co	Brownhills Pottery Co. (Tunstall, 1872–96)
B R & Co	Birks, Rawlins & Co. (Stoke, 1900–*c.* 1932)
B R & T	Baxter, Rowley & Tams (Longton, 1882–5)
B & S	Brown & Stevenson (Burslem, 1900–23)
B & S	Bishop & Stonier (Hanley 1890–1941)
B & Son	Bodley & Son (Burslem, 1882–7)
B & S H	B. and S. Hancock (Stoke, 1876–80)
B S & T	Barker, Sutton & Till (Burslem, 1834–43)
B & T	Blackhurst & Tunnicliffe (Burslem, 1879)
B W & B	Batkin, Walker & Broadhurst (Lane End, 1840–5)
B W & Co	Bates, Walker & Co. (Burslem, 1876–8)
B W M & Co	Brown-Westhead, Moore & Co. (Cauldon Place, Shelton, 1862–1904; also Hanley, 1872–1901)
C A L	Charles Amison (Longton, 1889–1916)
C B L	Collingwood Bros. (Longton, 1888–1949)
C & B	Cotton & Barlow (Longton, 1850–5)
C & Co	Cope & Co. (Longton, 1887–1946)
C & Co	Colclough & Co. (Longton, 1887–1928)
C & E H	Cartwright & Edwards (Longton, 1859–)

C E & M B	Cork, Edge & Malkin (Burslem, 1860–71)
C F in monogram	Charles Ford (Shelton, 1875–1913)
C & G	Copeland and Garrett (Stoke, 1833–47)
C & H late Hackwood	Cockson & Harding (Shelton, 1856–62)
C & H	Coggins & Hill (Longton, 1892–98)
C J M & Co	C. J. Mason & Co. (Longton, 1851–4; and Lane Delph, 1845–8)
C K	Charles Keeling (Shelton, 1822–5)
C M	Charles Meigh (Hanley, 1835–48)
C M S & P	Charles Meigh, Son & Pankhurst (Hanley, 1850)
C W	Charles Waine (Longton, 1892–1920)
C & W	Capper & Wood (Burslem, 1895–1904)
D B & Co	Davenport, Banks & Co. (Hanley, 1862–73)
D B & Co	Dunn, Bennett & Co. (Hanley, 1878–87; Burslem 1887–)
D P Co	Diamond Pottery Co. (Hanley, 1908–35)
D P Co	Dresden Porcelain Co. (Longton, 1896–1904)
E & B	Evans & Booth (Burslem, 1856–69)
E B	Edwards & Brown (Longton, 1882–1933)
E B & J E L	E. Bourne & Leigh (Fenton & Burslem, 1892–1939)
E & C C	E. & C. Challinor (Fenton, 1862–91)
E F B & Co	Edward Fisher, Bodley & Co. (Burslem, 1862–80) (E F B & Son, later)
E J B	E. J. Birch (Hanley, 1796–1813)
E J D B Burslem	E. J. D. Bodley (Burslem, 1875–92)
E K B	Elkin, Knight & Bridgwood (Fenton, 1827–40)
E M & Co	Edge, Malkin & Co (Burslem, 1870–1902)
E P Co	Empire Porcelain Co. (Longport, 1879–89; Hanley, 1896–)
E S & Co	Eardley, Spear & Co. (Tunstall, 1873)
E U & M	Ellis, Unwin & Mountford (Hanley, 1860)
E W & S	Enoch Wood & Sons (Burslem, 1818–46)

F C	F. Cartlidge (Longton, 1889–92)
F & H	Forester & Hume (Fenton, 1887–93)
F M	Francis Morley (Shelton, 1845–50)
F M & Co	Francis Morley & Co. (Hanley, 1850–56)
F & R	Ford & Riley (Burslem, 1882–93)
F & S B	Ford & Son (Burslem, 1893–)
F W & Co	F. Winkle & Co. (Stoke, 1891–*c.* 1932)
G B	Grimwade Bros. (Hanley, 1886–1900)
G B & Co	George Bennett & Co. (Stoke, 1894–1902)
G F B	G. F. Bowers (Brownhills, Tunstall, 1842–68)
G H & Co	Gater, Hall & Co. (Burslem, 1895–1943)
G J & Sons	George Jones & Sons (Stoke, 1873–1952)
G L B & Co Longton	G. L. Bentley & Co. (Longton, 1898–1912)
G P & Co	George Proctor & Co. (Longton, 1892–1939)
G & S Ltd Burslem	Gibson & Sons Ltd. (Burslem, 1885–)
G T M Stoke	George Thomas Mountford (Stoke, 1888–98)
G & W	Gildea & Walker (Burslem, 1881–6)
G W & Sons	George Warrilow & Sons (Longton, 1892–1941)
G W T & Sons	G. W. Turner & Sons (Tunstall, 1873–94)
H & A	Hammersley & Asbury (Longton, 1872–4)
H A & Co over a crown	Harvey Adams & Co. (Longton & Stoke, 1870–88)
H A & Co L	H. Aynsley & Co. (Longton, 1873–)
H B	Hines Bros. (Fenton, 1886–1915)
H & B	Harrop & Burgess (Hanley, 1895–1904)
H & C F	Hulme & Christie (Fenton, 1894–1902)
H & C over a crown	Hammersley & Co. (Longton, 1887–)
H & Co	Hill & Co. (Longton, 1889–1920)
H C Co	Hanley China Co. (Hanley, 1900–01)
H F	E. Hughes & Co. (Fenton, 1889–1940)
H & G late Harvey	Holland & Green (Longton, 1853–82)

H & G B	Heath & Greatbach (Burslem, 1891–94)
H H & M	Holdcroft, Hill & Mellor (Burslem, 1860–70)
H J C	H. J. Colclough (Longton, 1897–)
H & K Tunstall	Hollinshead & Kirkham (Tunstall, 1876–1956)
H & K	Hackwood & Keeling (Hanley, 1835–6)
H M W & Sons	H. M. Williamson & Sons (Longton, 1880–1941)
H P Co	Hanley Porcelain Co. (Hanley, 1892–9)
H P M	Holmes, Plant & Maydew (Burslem, 1876–85)
H & S	Hilditch & Son (Lane End, 1822–30)
H & S Longton	Holmes & Son (Longton, 1899–1904)
H & W	Hancock & Whittingham (Stoke, 1873–9)
H W & Co Longton	Hawley, Webberley & Co. (Longton, 1896–1903)
H W & Co	Hancock, Whittingham & Co. (Burslem, 1863–72)
J E B	John & Edward Baddeley (Shelton, 1784–1808)
J B	Jacob Baggaley (Burslem, 1880–6)
J B & Co	J. Bennett & Co. (Hanley, 1896–1901)
J B & S	James Broadhurst & Sons (Fenton, 1897–)
J B & S	J. Beech & Son (Longton, 1860–98)
J B & Son	J. Beech & Son (Longton, 1860–98)
J D & Co	J. Dimmock & Co. (Hanley, 1862–1904)
J.E & S	John Edwards & Son (Burslem, 1854–82)
J G late Mayer	James Gildea (Burslem, 1885–8)
J & G A L	J. & G. Alcock (Cobridge, 1839–46)
J G S & Co	John Goodwin, Stoddard & Co. (Fenton, 1899–1940)
J H	J. Holdcroft (Longton, 1872–1906)
J H C & Co Longton	J. H. Cope & Co. (Longton, 1887–1934)

J H W & Sons HANLEY	J. H. Weatherby & Sons (Hanley & Tunstall, 1892–)
J K LONGTON	James Kent (Longton, 1889–)
J M & Co	James Macintyre & Co. (Burslem, 1866–ceased since 1930)
J M & S	J. Meir & Son (Tunstall, 1841–97)
J M & S	Job Meigh & Son (Hanley, 1812–34)
J P L	John Proctor (Longton, 1843–6)
J R	John Ridgway (Shelton, 1830–40)
J R B & Co	John Ridgway, Bates & Co. (Shelton, 1856–8)
J R L	J. Rogers (Longport, 1814–36)
J R & Co	John Ridgway & Co. (Shelton, 1841–55)
J & R G	John & Robert Godwin (Cobridge, 1834–66)
J S & Co	J. Shore & Co. (Longton, 1887–1905)
J T	John Tams (Longton, 1875–1903)
J T H	John Thomas Hudden (Longton, 1859–85)
J W R	John & William Ridgway (Shelton, 1814–30)
J & W R	John & William Ridgway (Shelton, 1814–30)
J W & S	J. Wilson & Son (Fenton, 1898–1926)
K & B	King & Barrett (Burslem, 1898–1946)
K & Co	W. Kirby & Co. (Fenton, 1879–85)
K & Co B	Keeling & Co. (Burslem, 1886–*c.* 1937)
K & Co E	Kirkland & Co. (Etruria, 1892–)
K E B	King, Edge & Barrett (Burslem, 1897)
K E & Co	Knight, Elkin & Co. (Fenton, 1826–47)
K F A P Co	Kensington Fine Art Pottery Co. (Hanley, 1892–1902)
L E & S	Liddell Elliot & Son (Burslem, 1862–9)
L H L E	Lockett & Hulme (Lane End, 1822–6)
L P Co	Livesley, Powell & Co. (Hanley, 1851–65)
L P Co (on an oval garter)	Longton Porcelain Co. (Longton, 1892–1908)

L S	Lancaster & Sons (Hanley, 1900–)
M	Mintons (Stoke, *c.* 1840–50)
M & A	Morley & Ashworth (Hanley, 1860–2)
M & B	Minton & Boyle (Stoke, 1836–41)
M & Co	Moore & Co (Fenton, 1872–92)
M & Co	Minton & Co. (Stoke, 1841–44; 1847–76)
M & H	Minton & Hollins (Stoke, 1846–68)
M L & Co	Moore, Leason & Co. (Fenton, 1892–6)
M & M	Mayer & Maudesley (Burslem, 1837–8)
M N & Co Longton	McNeal & Co. (Longton, 1895–1906)
M & N	Mayer & Newbold (Lane End, 1817–33)
M S & Co	Myott, Son & Co. (Stoke & Cobridge, 1880–)
M W & Co	Massey, Wildblood & Co. (Longton, 1887–90)
M W & Co	Morgan, Wood & Co. (Burslem, 1860–70)
M W & H	Malkin, Walker & Hulse (Longton, 1858–64)
N W P Co Burslem	New Wharf Pottery Co. (Burslem, 1878–94)
O H E C L	Old Hall Earthenware Co. Ltd. (Hanley, 1861–86)
P & B	Powell & Bishop (Hanley, 1867–78)
P & B B	Price Bros. (Burslem, 1897–1903)
P B & Co.	Pinder, Bourne & Co. (Burslem, 1862–82)
P B & H	Pinder, Bourne & Hope (Burslem, 1851–62)
P B L	Plant Bros. (Longton, 1892–1907)
P B & S	Powell, Bishop & Stonier (Hanley, 1878–91)
PP	Pearl Pottery Co. Ltd. (Hanley, 1894–1936)
P & S L	R. Plant & Sons (Longton, 1896–1902)
P & U	Poole & Unwin (Longton, 1872–6)
P W & Co	Podmore, Walker & Co. (Tunstall, 1834–55)
R R HACKWOOD	William Ratcliffe (Hanley, 1831–40)
R & D	Redfern & Drakeford (Longton, 1892–1933)

R G S & Co	R. G. Scrivener & Co. (Hanley, 1870–83)
R H	Ralph Hammersley (Shelton, Burslem, Tunstall, 1822–85)
R H & S	Ralph Hammersley & Sons (Tunstall & Burslem, 1886–1905)
R H & S L P	R. H. & S. L. Plant (Longton, 1898–)
R H P & Co	R. H. Plant & Co. (Longton, 1881–98)
R & L	Robinson & Leadbeater (Stoke, 1865–86)
R & L Ltd	Robinson & Leadbeater Ltd. (Stoke, 1886–1924)
R & M	Ridgway & Morley (Shelton, 1842–4)
R M W & Co	Ridgway, Morley, Wear & Co. (Shelton, 1836–42)
R & N	Rowley & Newton (Longton, 1896–1901)
R S	Ralph Stevenson (Cobridge, 1810–32)
R S	Colclough & Co., "Royal Stanley" ware (Longton, 1887–1928)
R & S	Rigby & Stevenson (Hanley, 1895–1907)
R S & Co	Rathbone, Smith & Co. (Tunstall, 1884–97)
R & S L	Robinson & Son (Longton & Fenton, 1884–1904)
R S R	Ridgway, Sparkes & Ridgway (Shelton, 1873–9)
R S & S	R. Stevenson & Son (Cobridge, 1832–5)
R S W	R. Stevenson & Williams (Cobridge, first half of 19th century)
R V W	Richard Vernon Wildblood (Longton, 1887–8)
S A & Co	Samuel Alcock & Co. (Cobridge & Burslem, 1828–59)
S & B T	Smith & Binnall (Tunstall, 1897–1901)
S Bros.	Stubbs Bros. (Fenton, 1899–1908)
S B & S	Sampson Bridgwood & Sons (Longton, 1853–)
S C C	Star China Co. (Longton, 1900–20)
S C Co	Star China Co. (Longton, 1900–20)
S & F	Smith & Ford (Burlsem, 1895–9)

S F & Co	S. Fielding & Co. (Fenton, 1878–now at Stoke)
S H	Sampson Hancock (Tunstall and Stoke, 1858–90)
S H & S	Sampson Hancock & Sons (Stoke, 1891–c. 1936)
S J B	Samuel Johnson (Burslem, 1887–c. 1930)
S K & Co	S. Keeling & Co. (Hanley, 1840–50)
S & L	Stanley & Lambert (Longton, 1850–4)
S R	Samuel Radford (Longton, 1879–85; Fenton, 1885–1957)
S & S S	Shaw & Sons (Sandford, 1893–1910)
S S	Sampson Smith (Longton, 1846–60)
S S Ltd LONGTON	Sampson Smith Ltd. (Longton, 1860–)
S & V COBRIDGE	Sant & Vodrey (Cobridge, 1887–93)
T A & S G	T. A. & S. Green (Fenton, 1876–90)
T B	Thomas Bevington (Hanley, 1869–91)
T & B G	Thomas & Ben Godwin (Burslem, 1811–46)
T B & S	Thomas Booth & Sons (Tunstall, 1872–6)
T C LONGTON	Thomas Cone (Longton, 1892–)
T & C F	Thomas & Charles Ford (Hanley, 1854–74)
T F & S Ltd	Thomas Forester & Sons Ltd. (Longton, 1883–)
T G FENTON	Thomas Green (Fenton, 1848–58)
T G & F B	T. G. & F. Booth (Tunstall, 1883–90)
T & K L	Taylor & Kent (Longton, 1867–)
T & L	Tams & Lowe (Longton, 1865–74)
T M	Thomas Morris (Longton, 1898–1903)
T P L	T. P. Ledger (Longton, 1900–05)
T & R B	T. &. R. Boote, Burslem (1842–)
T R & Co	T. Rathbone & Co. (Tunstall, 1892–1924)

T R & P	Tundley, Rhodes & Pinder (Burslem, 1875–84)
T T Hanley	Thomas Twyford (Hanley, 1860–89)
T T	Taylor, Tunnicliffe & Co. (Hanley, 1868–75)
T W & Co	Thomas Wood & Co. (Burslem, 1879–ceased since 1930)
T W & Co	Thomas Wild & Co. (Longton, 1897–1904)
T W & S	Thomas Wood & Sons (Burslem, 1887–97)
U H P Co	Upper Hanley Pottery Co. (Hanley & Cobridge, 1895–1910)
U M & T	Unwin, Mountford & Taylor (Hanley, 1864)
U T & Co Hanley	U. Thomas & Co. (Hanley, 1889–1905)
W	Wardle & Co. (Hanley, 1871–84)
W A A & Co	William Alsager, Adderley & Co. (Longton, 1886–1905)
W A & Co	William Adams & Co. (Tunstall, Greenfield, 1836–)
W A & S	William Adams & Sons (Tunstall, Greengates, 1834–)
W B	William Brownfield (Cobridge, 1851–70)
W B HANLEY	William Bennett (Hanley, 1882–1937)
W & B	Wood & Baggaley (Burslem, 1870–80)
W & B	Wood& Brownfield (Cobridge, 1841–50)
W & B Ltd B	Wood & Barker Ltd. (Burslem, 1898–1903)
W B & S	William Brownfield & Sons (Cobridge, 1871–92)
W & Co	Whittaker, Heath & Co. (Hanley, 1892–8)
W & C FOLEY CHINA	Wileman & Co. (Fenton, 1892–1925)
W C & Co	Wood, Challinor & Co. (Tunstall, 1860–4)
W & E C	W. & E. Corn (Burslem & Longport, 1864–91)
W E W	W. E. Withinshaw (Burslem, 1873–8)
W F & R	Whittingham, Ford & Riley (Burslem, 1867–82)

W H	William Hudson (Longton, 1889–1941)
W & H	Wildblood & Heath (Longton, 1888–98)
W & H B	Wood & Hulme (Burslem, 1882–1905)
W H L H	W. H. Lockitt (Hanley, 1900–20)
W H & S L	Wildblood, Heath & Sons (Longton, 1889–1927)
W & J H	W. & J. Harding (Shelton, 1862–72)
W K & Co	William Kirkby & Co. (Fenton, 1879–85)
W & L	Wildblood & Ledgar (Longton, 1896–1900)
W L L	William Lowe (Longton, 1875–1930)
W & R STOKE ON TRENT	Wiltshaw & Robinson (Stoke, 1891–1957)
W R	William Ridgway (Hanley, 1834–56)
W R & Co	William Ridgway & Co. (Hanley, 1830–54)
W & Sons	H. M. Williamson & Sons (Longton, 1880–1941)
W R S & Co	William Ridgway Son & Co. (Hanley 1838–48)
W W B	Wooldridge & Walley (Burslem, 1899–1902)
W W & Co	W. Wood & Co. (Burslem, 1871–1932)
Y & B	Yale & Barker (Longton, 1841–53)
Z B & S	Zacharia, Boyle & Son (Hanley & Stoke, 1828–1850)

APPENDIX III

DESIGN REGISTRATIONS FOR SCENIC PATTERNS

The following is a list of the design registrations for scenic patterns, in the form of prints for plates or dishes, which were made at the Patent Office between 1839 and 1870. The list does not include prints which are mainly of a floral or heraldic character. The title and the description of the material are given in the instances where they are specified. Most of the registrations are made by firms in north Staffordshire; the locations are stated in the case of firms or agents situated elsewhere.

1840 John Ridgway.
1841 J. & T. Edwards.
1842 Joseph Clementson (1), "Lucerne", Granite ware.
(2), "Rustic Scenery", Granite Opaque Pearl.
1843 Josiah Wedgwood & Sons, "Windmill".
1844 Thomas Dimmock, Jnr., "Rhine", Kaolin ware.
John Ridgway, "Doria", Stone.
J. K. Knight & G. Elkin, "Baronial Halls" / "Cobham Hall".
Clementson, Young & Jameson, "Aleppo", Ironstone.
James Edwards.
Copeland & Garrett.
William Ridgway & Son.
John Meir & Son, "Mazara", Ironstone.
1845 George Phillips, "Corinth", Ironstone.
Jacob Furnival (1).
Enoch Wood & Sons, "Lucerne".
William Adams & Sons, "Habana".
Jacob Furnival (2).
Copeland & Garrett.

1846 Joseph Clementson, "Tessino", Ironstone.
John Goodwin (1).
John Ridgway, "Aladdin".
George Phillips (1).
Copeland & Garrett.
George Phillips (2), "Friburg", Ironstone.
John Goodwin (2), "Rousillon", Ironstone.
Edward Challinor, "Soiro", Ironstone.

1847 John Wedgwood.
John Ridgway.
Mellor, Venables & Co., "Medici".

1848 John Wedgwood.
John Meir & Son.
W. T. Copeland.
John Ridgway.

1849 William Adams & Sons, "Athens", Ironstone.
Joseph Clementson.
Josiah Wedgwood & Sons, "California", Pearl Stone Ware.
John Wedgwood.
Mellor, Venables & Co., "Windsor".

1850 J. & M. P. Bell (Glasgow) (1), "Iona".
Joseph Clementson, "Siam", Ironstone.
J. & M. P. Bell (Glasgow) (2), "Warwick Vase".
Barker & Son, "Missouri".
John Ridgway (1) and (2).
W. T. Copeland.

1851 W. T. Copeland (1) and (2).
R. Britton (Leeds).

1852 William & George Harding.
Venables & Baines.
Marple, Turner & Co.
John Holland.

1853 Minton.
George Wooliscroft, "Eon", Ironstone.
Anthony Shaw.
William Adams & Sons.

1854 John Ridgway, "Byzantium".

1855 Samuel Alcock, "British Birds".

1856 Joseph Clementson, "Claremont", Ironstone.
Edward Challinor, "Dora".
1857 W. T. Copeland.
1858 Anthony Shaw, "Castanette Dance".
1860 John Wedgwood.
1861 J. & J. Peake.
1862 William Brownfield.
Eardley & Hammersley.
Edward Challinor.
Jones & Ellis.
1863 Bodley & Harrold (1), "The Princess Alexandra".
Bodley & Harrold (2).
1864 George L. Ashworth & Brothers.
Hope & Carter (1) and (2).
1865 Hope & Carter (1), "Horse Hunt".
(2), "Odessa".
Thomas Till & Sons.
Hill Pottery Company.
Antonio John Claddo (Birmingham), (Islamic inscription).
1866 Burgess & Leigh, "Barbarini Vase".
Ford, Challinor & Co.
Walker & Carter, "Roumelia".
George L. Ashworth & Brothers, "St. Petersburg" (Russian inscription).
1867 George L. Ashworth & Brothers, "Seasons".
Hope & Carter, "Ballet".
John Wedgwood, "Woronzoff", Patent TP Paris White Ironstone.
Ford & Challinor (1) "Monument" (Russian inscription).
(2), "Russian views".
1868 Cork, Edge & Malkin, "Theatre" (Russian inscription).
Hope & Carter, "Mexico".
Carpi, Loly & Co. (Liverpool) (1), "The King and Queen of Greece" (Greek inscription).
(2), (Greek inscription).
Holdcroft & Wood, "Napoleon à Fontainebleau".
Edward F. Bodley, "Bonaparte".
Ralph Malkin (Rumanian inscription).

1868 John Wedgwood, "Alexander".
Thomas Booth.
1869 F. Primavesi & Sons (Cardiff) (1) and (2).
Wood & Piggot, "Wien".
(?) Trachtenberg & Panthes (Odessa), "Kieff".
Charles Stanley (near Rotherham).
John Pratt.
1870 Cork, Edge & Malkin.
C. D. Christodulo (?).

APPENDIX IV

MINTON DATE MARKS

From 1842 a system of year cyphers and month letters was used on Minton ware, as listed at (*a*) and (*b*) below. These were usually accompanied by the personal mark of the potter. From about 1862 the name MINTON was added, and from about 1872 this was rendered as MINTONS. These marks were impressed, and in consequence refer to the potting of a piece and not to its decoration.

(*a*)

1842	1843	1844	1845	1846	1847	1848	1849
1850	1851	1852	1853	1854	1855	1856	1857
1858	1859	1860	1861	1862	1863	1864	1865
1866	1867	1868	1869	1870	1871	1872	1873
1874	1875	1876	1877	1878	1879	1880	1881
1882	1883	1884	1885	1886	1887	1888	1889
1890	1891	1892	1893	1894	1895	1896	1897
1898	1899	1900	1901	1902	1903	1904	1905

(*b*)

J — January	H — July
F — February	Y — August
M — March	S — September
A — April	O — October
E — May	N — November
I — June	D — December

APPENDIX V

WEDGWOOD DATE MARKS

From 1860 a system of date marks was used on Wedgwood ware consisting of three capital letters impressed side by side. The first indicated the month according to codes (*a*) and (*b*) below. The second was the personal mark of the potter. The third indicated the year of manufacture according to the codes (*c*), (*d*) and (*e*).

It will be noticed that with this system there was no means of distinguishing between the different cycles of year marks. This was rectified in 1907 by the substitution of the number of the cycle for the month letter; and the system was again changed in 1930 when the cycle number was replaced by the chronological number of the month and the year was indicated by the last two numbers of the actual date.

(*a*) Month letters from 1860 to 1864:

J — January
F — February
M — March
A — April
Y — May
T — June
V — July
W — August
S — September
O — October
N — November
D — December

(*b*) Month letters from 1865 to 1907:

J — January
F — February
R — March
A — April
M — May
T — June
L — July
W — August
S — September
O — October
N — November
D — December

(*c*) Year letters from 1860 to 1871:

O — 1860
P — 1861
Q — 1862
R — 1863
S — 1864
T — 1865
U — 1866
V — 1867
W — 1868
X — 1869
Y — 1870
Z — 1871

94. Green-glazed slipware dish with sgraffito decoration, made by Edwin B. Fishley, Fremington. Signed on the underside and dated 1897. Diam. 11 in.
Victoria & Albert Museum.

95
Puzzle jug from Buckley, Flintshire, with slip inscripti
'Isaac Connah 1875'. Ht. $7\frac{1}{4}$ in. *Grosvenor Museum, Chester.*

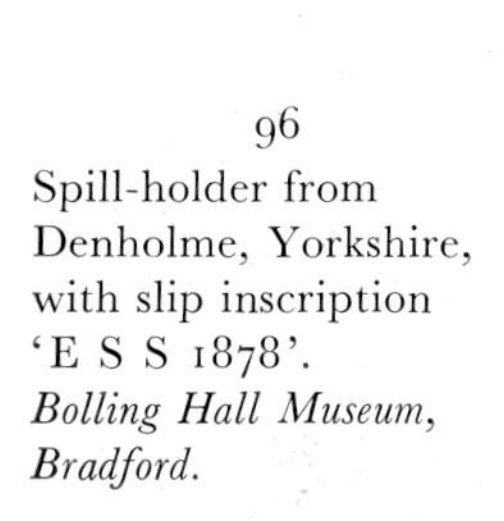

96
Spill-holder from Denholme, Yorkshire, with slip inscription 'E S S 1878'. *Bolling Hall Museum, Bradford.*

97. Teapot of red earthenware, with applied decoration in white clay partly painted with green glaze, made by Edward Bingham, Castle Hedingham, in the late nineteenth century. On the lid and beside the handle are the marks of a castle and the monogram E B. Ht. 8½ in. *Victoria & Albert Museum*

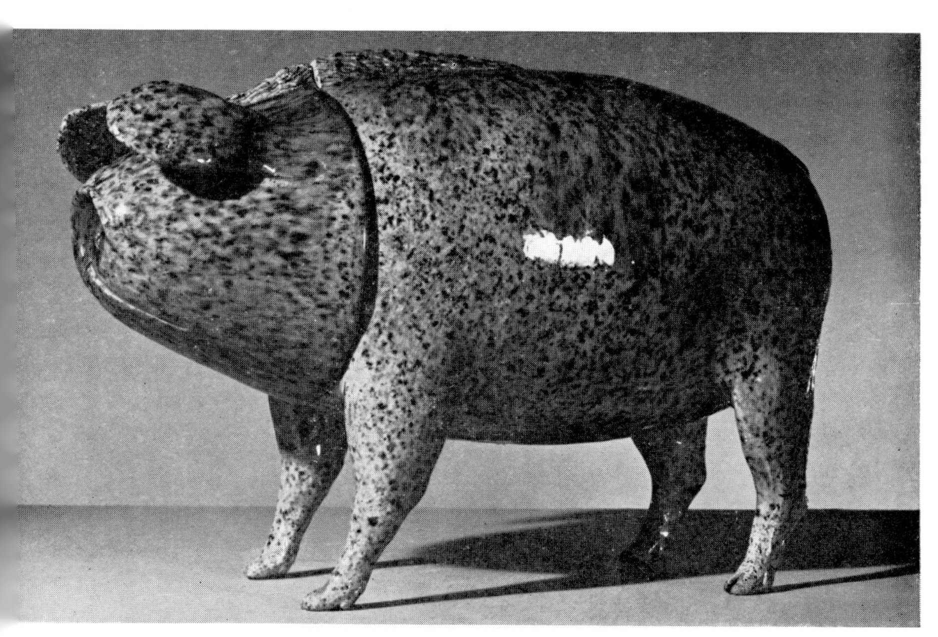

98. 'Sussex pig' with detachable head, finished with a splashed glaze. Length 10⅛ in. *Victoria & Albert Museum.*

99. Teapot with applied coloured decoration on a brown ground. Made in South Derbyshire in the late nineteenth century. Ht. 13 in. *Victoria & Albert Museum.*

(*d*) Year letters from 1872 to 1897:

A — 1872	J — 1881	S — 1890
B — 1873	K — 1882	T — 1891
C — 1874	L — 1883	U — 1892
D — 1875	M — 1884	V — 1893
E — 1876	N — 1885	W — 1894
F — 1877	O — 1886	X — 1895
G — 1878	P — 1887	Y — 1896
H — 1879	Q — 1888	Z — 1897
I — 1880	R — 1889	

(*e*) Year letters from 1898:

A — 1898	C — 1900	E — 1902
B — 1899	D — 1901	etc.

APPENDIX VI

ARTIST'S MARKS USED AT DOULTONS LAMBETH

(a) The following are all listed in John Sparkes' lectures of 1874 and 1880 to the Society of Arts:

(i) Stoneware:

Hannah B. Barlow

Eliza (or Elise) Simance

(This mark is reproduced, with a later version, from Blacker—see below)

Florence E. Barlow

(This mark is reproduced, with a later version, from Blacker—see below)

Eliza S. Banks

Emily J. Edwards

Louisa E. Edwards

Arthur B. Barlow

Louisa J. Davis

Frank A. Butler

Edith D. Lupton

George Tinworth 

Frances E. Lee

Mary Mitchell

(ii) Faience and Impasto ware:

Florence Lewis 

Mary Butterton 

Isabel Lewis 

Alice Shelly 

Miss M. L. Crawley 

Euphemia A. Thatcher 

Mary Capes 

Esther Lewis 

Katherine Sturgeon 

Linnie Watt 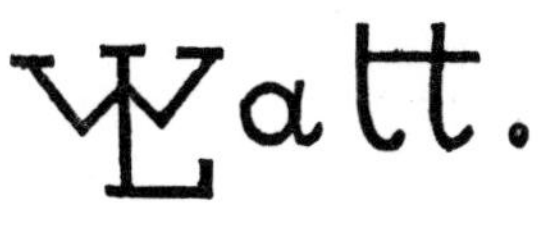

Fanny Stable 

Miss Linnell 

All under this heading were listed for their work on the faience, excepting Miss Linnell and her predecessor Miss F. M. Collins (Mrs. Vale) who were concerned with impasto ware. The latter's mark was not specified. The following, whose marks were also not specified, worked on faience: Mary Armstrong, Alberta Green, Matilda Adams, Margaret Challis, Helen A. Arding and Miss M. M. Arding.

(b) The following additional marks were listed by J. F. Blacker in *The ABC of English Salt-glaze Stoneware*, (1922), with the exception of Katharine B. Smallfield whose work of about 1884 is represented in the Victoria and Albert Museum.

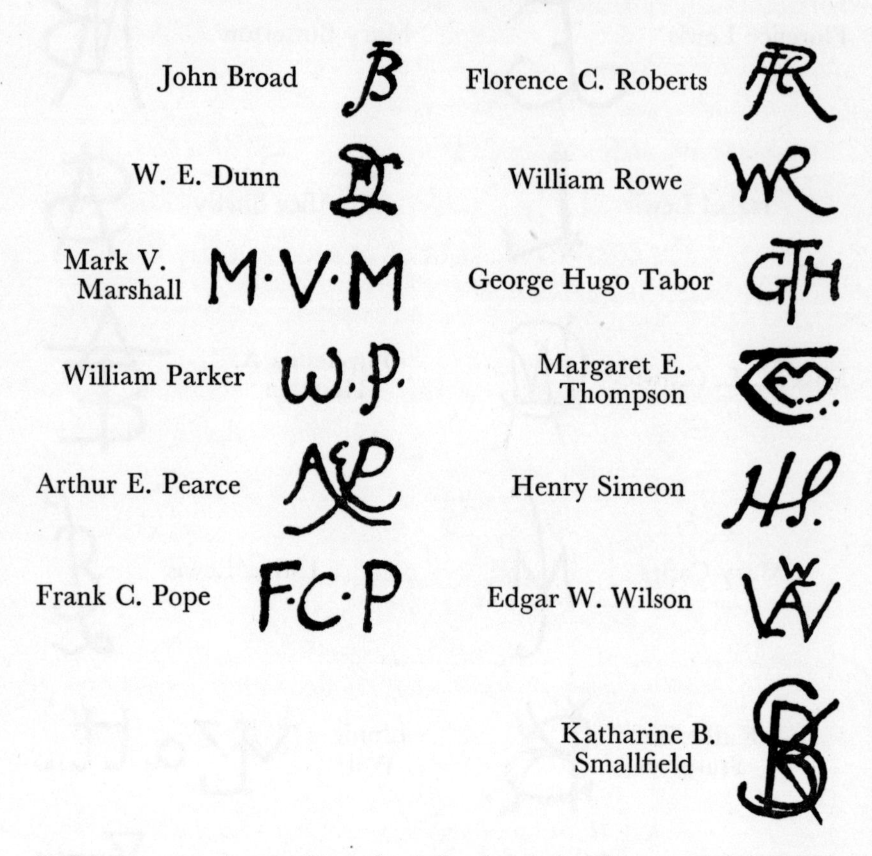

Reference was also made to the following artists in an article of May 1887 in the *Journal of Decorative Art*: Miss Denley, Miss A. Dennis, J. Eyre, Miss E. D. Leefton, M. E. Roberts and Miss Kate Rogers.

APPENDIX VII

MARKS ON MARTIN BROTHERS POTTERY (based on C. R. Beard, *Catalogue of Martinware in the possession of F. J. Nettlefold*, London, 1936, but incorporating additional material).

Form of signature (All are signed by hand in the wet clay except where otherwise stated).

1873–4: *R. W. Martin, Fulham.*
Variation: *Pomona House, Fulham, 1873.*

1874–7: *R. W. Martin, London.*
Variations: *Martin, London.*
R. W. MARTIN, LONDON.
FECIT R. W. MARTIN (impressed).

1877–8: *R. W. Martin, Southall.*
Variations: *Southall Pottery.*
MARTIN, SOUTHALL POTTERY (oval stamp).
R. W. MARTIN, SOUTHALL (impressed).
R. Wallace Martin Sc., Southall (also in capitals) (noted on figures).

1879–*c.* 1883: *R. W. Martin, London & Southall.*
Variations: *Martin, London & Southall.*
R. W. Martin, London (in addition to normal signature).

c. 1883–1914: *R. W. Martin & Bros.* (or *Brothers*), *London & Southall* or *Martin Bros.* (or *Brothers*), *London & Southall.*
Variations: *Martin Bros., London.*
R. W. Martin, London & Southall.
RWM (in monogram), *Southall* (in addition to
RWM Sc. normal signature on figures)

1914: *R. W. Martin & Bros., Southall* or *Martin Bros., Southall* (one example noted with initials EBM for Edwin Martin)

Serial number and dates. (The serial numbers seem to appear only on vessels, and not on figures.)

1873–4 a serial number, or a serial letter and number; often dated.

1874–5: a serial letter and number; usually dated.

Late 1875–*c.* 1880: a serial number (without letter); usually dated.

c. 1880 onwards: no serial number; usually dated.

APPENDIX VIII

MARKS ON DE MORGAN POTTERY AND TILES (based on *Catalogue of Works by William De Morgan*, Victoria and Albert Museum [1921]), with additional material. The marks are not drawn to scale.

(*a*) 

Perhaps Chelsea period, previous to 1882.

(*b*) 

Merton Abbey period, 1882–8.

(*c*) 

As above.

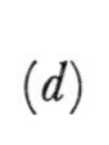
(*d*) 

As above.

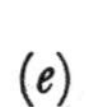
(*e*) 

Early Fulham period, De Morgan in partnership with Halsey Ricardo 1888–98.

(*f*) 

As above.

(*g*) 

As above.

(*h*) 

As above.

(*i*) 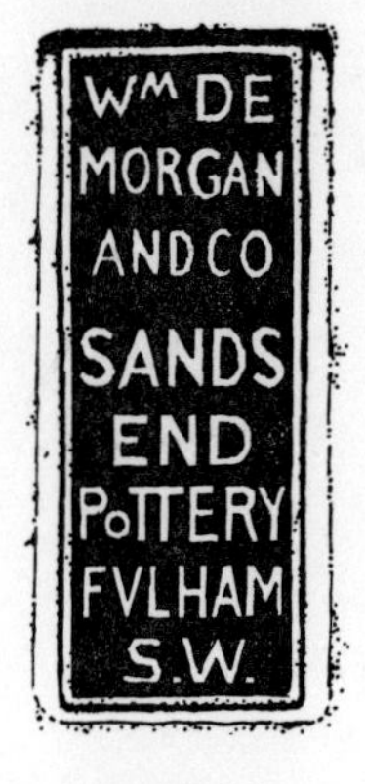

Later Fulham period, De Morgan in partnership with Iles and the two Passengers, 1898–1907.

(*j*) 

As above.

(*k*) 

As above.

(*l*) 

Denotes work painted by Fred Passenger at Bushey Heath, 1921–33.

All of the marks above are impressed in the clay, with the exception of (*l*) which may be impressed or printed.

In addition, or as an alternative, hand-painted marks often occur, especially on pottery of the Fulham period. These are commonly, but not invariably, in capitals with the name spelled out according to space: D. M. FULHAM, W.D.M. FULHAM, DE MORGAN FULHAM, W. DE MORGAN FULHAM.

The painted initials of the individual decorators are also common on the later pottery:

F P	— Fred Passenger	C P	— Charles Passenger
J J	— Joe Juster	J H	— J. Hersey

SHORT BIBLIOGRAPHY

Ceramic Art of Great Britain. L. Jewitt. 1877 (2nd edition 1883).

Staffordshire Pots and Potters. G. W. & F. A. Rhead. 1906.

Nineteenth-Century English Ceramic Art. J. F. Blacker. 1911.

Yorkshire Potteries, Pots and Potters (Yorkshire Philosophical Society Annual Report, 1915). O. Grabham.

Catalogue of Works by William De Morgan. Victoria and Albert Museum. 1921.

The ABC of English Salt-glaze Stoneware from Dwight to Doulton. J. F. Blacker. 1922.

William De Morgan and his Wife. A. M. W. Stirling. 1922.

Catalogue of the Collection of Martinware formed by Mr. Frederick John Nettlefold. C. R. Beard. 1936.

American Historical Views on Staffordshire China. E. B. Larsen. 1939.

Sussex Pottery (Pt. 1: East Sussex). (Hastings Museum publication). J. M. Baines. 1948.

Under-glaze Colour Picture Prints on Staffordshire Pottery. H. G. Clarke. 1949.

English Country Pottery. R. G. Haggar. 1950.

Nineteenth Century English Pottery and Porcelain. G. Bemrose. 1952.

Victorian and Edwardian Decorative Arts. Victoria and Albert Museum exhibition catalogue. 1952.

Staffordshire Chimney Ornaments. R. G. Haggar. 1955.

Handbook of Pottery and Porcelain Marks. J. P. Cushion & W. B. Honey. 1956 (2nd edition 1958).

Concise Encyclopaedia of English Pottery and Porcelain. W. Mankowitz & R. G. Haggar. 1957.

Staffordshire Portrait Figures of the Victorian Age. T. Balston. 1958.

Connoisseur Period Guide: Early Victorian. Chapter on "Pottery, Porcelain and Glass" by H. Wakefield. 1958.

Connoisseur Concise Encyclopaedia of Antiques. Vol. IV. Article on "English Ceramic Artists of the Victorian Era" by G. Godden. 1959.

Victorian Pottery and Porcelain. G. B. Hughes. 1959.

The Potteries of Sunderland and District. Sunderland Museum and Art Gallery. (2nd edition 1961).

INDEX

The index does not contain references to the list of firms classified by initials in Appendix II.

F

G

H

I

J

K

L